DEVASTATION iN MOUNTAIN MEASURE

Bringing Victory from Sorrow:
A Story of God's Faithfulness

DEVASTATION iN MOUNTAIN MEASURE

MARION ZIRKLE WRIGHT

REDEMPTION PRESS

The author has tried to recreate events, locales, and
conversations from her memories of them. In order to maintain
their anonymity, in some instances she has changed the
names of individuals and may have changed some identifying
characteristics and details, such as physical properties,
occupations, and places of residence.

Unless otherwise indicated, all Scripture quotations are taken
from the New King James Version®. Copyright © 1982 by
Thomas Nelson. Used by permission. All rights reserved.

Scripture quotations marked (KJV) are taken from the King
James Version, public domain.

ISBN 13: 978-1-64645-515-7 (Paperbook)
        978-1-64645-516-4 (ePub)
        978-1-64645-517-1 (Mobi)

LCCN: 2022903722

DEDICATION

To my husband, Clarence Wright, who believes in me and believes in what the Lord has called me to do. He adds so much strength to my life.

To my beautiful daughters, Kimberly Zirkle Mejia (and husband Dany Mejia) and Deborah Zirkle Spanberger (and husband Keith), who have loved me and brought great joy to my life. They have been my cheerleaders through the thick and the thin.

To my precious son, Jimmy, so dearly loved, and who waits for me in heaven.

To my wonderful and delightful grandchildren, whom I love with a depth I can't explain: Christopher, Marion (and husband Kyle), Ashley (and husband Joshua), Matthew, Ricky (and wife Harley), Lynsey (and husband Rafael), Jimmy (and wife Erika), Alexis (and husband Sam), Parker (and wife Brandie), Jordan (and wife Bailey), Adrienne, and Daniela.

To my great-grandchildren, who have blessed me beyond measure and filled my heart with joy and love to overflowing: Vincent Gabriel, Isabella Sofia, Alex Michael, Gabriel Paul, Elliot Samuel,

Jeremiah James, Sophia Kay, Emersyn Kate, Elihu James, Ada Jane, Owen John, and Vanessa Joy.

As I finalized the writing of this book, my beautiful sister, Linda, went home to be with the Lord on Sunday, August 22, 2021, in Louisville, Kentucky. We had seventy-five wonderful years to share together. I have a heart full of precious memories from the time we were little girls playing house until we had grandchildren. I loved my sister deeply. We could talk about anything, share our secrets and desires, and have some disagreements. But we could disagree without being disagreeable. I miss her more than I can put into words, but I know that I will see her again and spend all eternity with her.

My sister, Linda McNabb

CONTENTS

ACKNOWLEDGMENTS

I would like to thank Gregg Ford, who encouraged me to write this book and gave me the first offerings toward the printing costs.

A big thanks goes to Kate Gutierrez, who spent hours reading, editing, and rereading the first draft.

Also, thanks to my daughters, Kimberly and Debbie, who helped me remember many details.

ACKNOWLEDGEMENTS

FOREWORD

It seems like only yesterday that the Lord Jesus directed me to call Dr. Jim and Marion Zirkle and partner with Living Water Teaching Ministries.

Many years ago now, I was blessed and honored to meet with Jim and hand him a check for $300,000.00—Kenneth Copeland Ministries' first large mission seed in its history. I will never forget that day. Our ministry and theirs were joined together in an everlasting covenant to reach all of Guatemala and beyond with the Word of faith and the love of Jesus.

I had first met Jim and Marion through Kenneth Hagin and Rhema Bible Training Center. But now, this powerful joining brought us together as a teaching, preaching, and healing team the likes of which I had never been a part of.

Through this covenant joining, I have had the privilege of ministering the Word there in Guatemala. The Lord began to bless KCM financially to the point that we were able to purchase a brand-new, single-engine Cessna airplane and station it there.

Jim and Marion had been driving hours just to get around and through the mountains. Now they could fly over the mountains and the dangerous rebel strongholds to minister to the people in minutes. It was absolutely fabulous!

They very soon outgrew the little Cessna, so the next step was the Douglas DC-3. It was absolutely wonderful! It had the capacity to haul huge amounts of cargo and people. They could load up and fly over the mountains, unload, and then go back and repeat the process with tons of life-saving goods, and most importantly, the Word of God. It worked!

And then came that terrible, awful day. But thank God for victory over death! And now, think about it. Forty years have gone by, and Living Water Teaching is stronger than ever. Guatemala has gone through changes that only the power of God could have brought to pass.

As you read Marion's personal account of this miraculous journey, you will laugh, cry, shout, and most of all, be blessed and healed at the same time.

Jesus is Lord!

Kenneth Copeland

1

A MEDICAL CAMPAIGN: A TOOL FOR EVANGELISM

Winning the lost, one soul at a time, is the desired outcome of every mission endeavor that we have. Every March and October, Living Water Teaching, the ministry my husband Jim and I founded in Guatemala, sets up a medical clinic, which serves as an evangelistic tool to bring people to the Lord. One of these clinics, which was held in Playa Grande in 1998, proved to be one of our most successful clinics ever, as we saw over fifteen hundred people come to know the Lord. But it also ended in the death of eleven people, including my dear husband, son, and son-in-law.

We treat thousands of patients at our medical clinics, and they are massive efforts for both our staff and our volunteer teams. We send two or three staff members ahead of a campaign to check out the designated area chosen due to its limited medicine, doctors, and nurses. Our staff talk with local pastors, who help get the word out. The team looks for a place big enough to have the clinic, a place to sleep, and a means of fixing meals. In areas without hotels, we ask the local pastors if they would be willing to let our group sleep on the church floor with sleeping bags, cots, or air mattresses. The local pastors are always willing to help, especially since their people can visit the clinic and receive free medical checkups and medicine. After firming up the location, we fill in the rest of the team and get everybody on board: group leaders, missionaries, and our trip coordinator in the Caddo Mills, Texas, office.

Living Water Teaching is involved in multiple outreaches, so at the end of each year, we set our dates for the next year's activities: medical outreaches in March and October, summer visits from two or three youth teams, Bible school graduation, two seminars, and our Christmas outreach (Operation Shoebox) for youth and children.

Our trip coordinator is in charge of calling churches to line up volunteers for the medical trips. Some of our group members have participated in forty or fifty outreaches. Some bring friends who don't attend church so they, too, can have a mission experience. Over the years, hundreds of pastors have participated in these medical trips, and we invite the pastors to preach in the night services. It is an added blessing when doctors, dentists, or nurses join us. If not, we use local medical and dental personnel and give them an offering.

All group attendees pay for their trip at least one month before the outreach. That way, we can buy food, fill vehicles with gas, and buy insurance.

In October 1998, we planned a medical/evangelistic campaign in Playa Grande in the northern part of Guatemala. One of our largest volunteer groups ever of about 105 people from several states flew down from the United States to help us. Included in this group were two sons-in-law, Keith Spanberger and Chris Hamberger. A team of missionaries and staff drove for two days from our Bible school campus in Quetzaltenango (most people use the Indian name "Xela" instead of Quetzaltenango) to the medical campaign site. They were ready to bring trucks filled with food, kitchen items, medical equipment, enough medicine for a three-day clinic, dental chairs, and a generator in case the electricity goes off. They had their suitcases and sleeping bags, along with microphones, Bibles, and teaching tracts.

Our team from Quetzaltenango (Xela) arrived first and set up the campaign site: a makeshift kitchen, a pharmacy with medication, exam rooms for the doctors and the dentists, and prayer areas. Then they cleaned all the rooms for the group arriving from the United States.

My husband Jim and I met the group in Guatemala City to fly on to Playa Grande. My son, Jimmy, flew our DC-3 aircraft with some group members. A pilot with the military flew another DC-3 with group members during the forty-five-minute flight.

Everyone was excited, with people talking and laughing. We're always glad to have first-time workers, but many on this trip had been here before, so they greeted and hugged people they remembered from other medical trips. After we arrived in Playa Grande, some soldiers welcomed us, and then we loaded up in military trucks and made the trek to the medical site a few miles away.

The missionaries and staff from Quetzaltenango welcomed the group members. Our ministry leaders showed the newcomers to their rooms where volunteers would be sleeping in bunkbeds, air mattresses, or little tents. Everybody was given their schedule and assignment for the next three days. We were blessed to have several doctors, dentists, and nurses on this trip.

On the clinic's first day, people arrived at around four in the morning, and the line stretched as far as the eye could see. Visitors remained patient during the long, three-hour wait because they were grateful to have access to doctors, dentists, and free medicine and vitamins. Many mothers carried their babies on their backs in makeshift slings, pulling other little ones alongside them. Old men, young men, grandmas, young girls, and hundreds of children stood in line to see the people who would take care of their medical needs.

By the time the sun rose, it was hot, and the people had already stood in line for hours. Babies cried, wanting to nurse, little children were restless and hungry, and the people were tired.

We served breakfast around seven o'clock to the entire ministry team, had a time of worship and prayer, and then at eight, the whole team took their places, ready to open the clinic.

Two Spanish-speaking volunteers took the patients' histories, finding out patients' names and ages, noting where they lived and what they came for. We formed three lines—one for the doctors, one for the dentists, and one for the chiropractors. A team member led guests to the right area. After their examination, another team member showed them to the pharmacy and then to the prayer area.

At all of our medical clinics, every person who passes through must enter the prayer station before they can leave. The gospel is presented to those who do not know the Lord, and hands are laid on each person for healing. I always work in this area of the clinic. I have had the opportunity to lead a few thousand people to the Lord.

We give a Spanish New Testament to each person who accepts Jesus in the clinic if they do not have one at home. Then we write down their names and addresses, and we leave these papers in the hands of the local pastors for follow-up. We also give teaching tracts to all those who come through the clinic, including children's tracts with pictures when we have those available.

On the second day of this clinic, Hurricane Mitch dropped barrels of water, but it didn't stop several thousand people from coming over the three days. We saw every kind of ailment and sickness imaginable. One person was carried in on a stretcher. Some had rotten teeth, and others had no teeth. Many people came without shoes, and the stench of body odor was strong. Some people's breath was so bad, we had to turn away when we prayed for them. The prayer area was set up outside in a tent with open sides because it was so hot, and it was the final area the people came through before leaving for home.

During breaks in the weather, we looked for brooms to prop up the tent and dispel the water. The prayer area soon had a mud floor. Still the people came. A little nearby creek rose rapidly in the continual downpour. On Friday, the third and last day of the clinic, more rain fell.

However, the sun came out in the afternoon, so Jim thought it wise to begin flying the US group to our Bible school campus in Quetzaltenango. It was a forty-five-minute flight. The first group of twenty-six left in our Douglas DC-3 aircraft for our ministry facilities. Tom VanderPol was the pilot, and my son, Jimmy, was the copilot.

We had treated close to seven thousand people, and approximately fifteen hundred had received Jesus as their Savior. The campaign had been very fruitful!

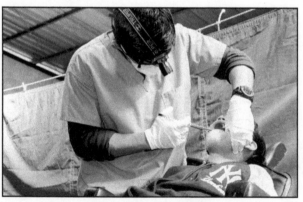

Medical campaign

At three o'clock Saturday morning, the missionaries and staff began their long drive home. After breakfast, Jim asked me to fly to our ministry facilities in Quetzaltenango with the second group of about twenty-six people from the United States.

Jim and I had no idea this would be our last time together. We hugged and kissed as we always did and said something like, "I'll see you back in Xela." I didn't sense anything in my spirit that made me think I might not see him the next day.

The sun shone that Saturday morning as we left Playa Grande. I sat up front in the jump seat between Jimmy and Tom. I was very proud that my son was living his dream. He loved flying, and he loved his work for the Lord.

We had to land in Guatemala City, the capital, because we found out that the Xela airport was socked in. This meant we were grounded because of a low cloud cover. The Xela airport had no terminal, so our pilots always flew VFR (visual flight rules). These rules govern the operation of aircraft using visual meteorological conditions. In other words, the pilot must be able to see the dirt runway in order to land. Sometimes someone from our ministry had to drive down the runway, shoo the cows off it, and tell the people crossing over that an aircraft was coming in.

Jimmy and Tom landed the plane in Guatemala City and unloaded the twenty-six group members from the airplane into our Toyota Coaster that was already in Guatemala City. Then, with our ministry's legal representative, Julio Aceituno, at the wheel, we drove five to six hours to our home.

Waiting for the bus to load, I saw my precious son alive for the last time.

I remember hugging him as I always did. He looked so handsome in his pilot shirt. I told him that I loved him and would see him in Xela. Jimmy meant more to me than life itself. He was just thirty years old and was a loving husband, father of four children, minister of the gospel, pilot, and director of our ministry.

En route to Xela, the bus's brakes locked up. We called Guatemala City and asked Tom, the copilot and mechanic, to come and figure out the problem. He and Jimmy were spending the night in Guatemala City before flying back into Playa Grande the next morning to bring more group members to our campus in Xela.

Tom fixed the brakes, and then he drove to Xela with us, arriving in the middle of the night. His wife, Renae, waited up to settle the group members into their accommodations for the night. Little did Tom know that this would be the last night he would see his precious wife, Renae, pregnant with their second baby, or their little girl, Shayla.

2

THE ACCiDENT

On Sunday, November 1, 1998, at around two o'clock in the afternoon, my life changed forever.

I had returned from our local church, where we had just celebrated our eleventh anniversary that morning. I fixed myself some lunch. The rain had finally stopped, and the beautiful sun had appeared. I walked across the yard to see if my daughter-in-law, Laura, had heard anything from Jimmy.

I received a phone call from one of our guards, telling me that our airplane had crashed a few miles from our Bible school campus in Xela. I could not believe what I was hearing. I wanted to cry out, "No, no, no!" But my little four-year-old grandson, Jimmy, sat in the floor in front of me, playing with his toys. I leaned closer to Laura and whispered, "The plane has crashed."

I ran as fast as I could to my house to ask J. D., a team member who was staying with us, to ride to the airport with Laura and me. Meanwhile, Laura arranged for a staff member to take care of her one-year-old son, Jordan, two-year-old daughter, Alexis, and four-year-old Jimmy.

J. D. took the wheel, and I rode up front with him. We stopped and picked up one of our guards and took off at top speed for the airport, about a fifteen-minute ride. We drove down the whole dirt runway with no plane in sight. We saw some deep ruts where our third group had landed, returning from Playa Grande.

As we left the airport, we asked some bystanders if they'd heard about a plane crash. They had, and they pointed us in the right direction. We checked with other people along the way, and they confirmed the location. Shortly, we saw one of our ministry vehicles climbing the mountain and carrying several of the pastors and group members who had been on the trip, so we followed them.

My heart cried out, *Lord, please let my husband and son be alive.*

Laura was quiet in the back seat, a hundred dreadful thoughts surely racing through her mind. Because of the mud, we had to leave the car at the bottom of the mountain and head up on foot. Hurricane Mitch had pelted us with rain off and on for several days, so we slipped and slid our way up the mountain. Our guard held onto me to keep me from falling, and J. D. and Laura climbed close by.

As we ascended the mountain, we met other climbers who had heard horror stories of mutilated bodies. At one point as I trudged up the mountain, I looked back, and Laura was nowhere in sight. She told me later that she knew Jimmy—her husband and my son—had not made it. She went back down the mountain and home to be with her three precious children, her heart heavy as she waited for more news.

Mud covered my shoes, making my feet so heavy I could barely pick them up, but our guard pulled me along. My adrenaline flowed and my heart beat wildly as I held onto hope that my husband and son were still alive. Many people stood outside their homes—some in small groups, others talking loudly, some no doubt praying because of the devastation they had seen. Their faces filled with horror, they watched us climb the mountain, knowing what awaited us. We sunk down in mud over our shoes. Trees had fallen everywhere, and Hurricane Mitch had scattered broken limbs over the hillside. It looked like a cyclone had just left the area with debris strewn all over the place.

It was about three in the afternoon; the sun was out and hot after hours and hours of falling rain. After what seemed like an hour, we saw the aircraft, now in pieces and guarded by the military. There were plane parts covering most of the mountain terrain, along with personal items, clothing, and so much more as suitcases had been thrown around and broken open during the impact.

"My husband and son were on this aircraft," I cried out to the soldier nearest me.

He merely stepped out of the way as he looked into the face of this distraught woman.

The first thing I saw was a passport on the stacked bodies. I picked it up and opened it. I felt the blood drain from my face as I gazed at the picture inside.

It was Jim. My husband.

Part of me wanted to toss it into the mud. Maybe if I couldn't see it, Jim would still be alive. But logic took over, and I slipped it into my purse.

Gathering all my strength and breathing a prayer—for what, I don't remember—I took in the scene. I saw several bodies. Four of them were group members. The soldiers had stacked them one on top of the other inside the wreckage.

It was hard for me to believe what I saw. *Lord, just a few hours ago, these precious people were alive and working diligently to be a blessing to others and now . . .*

I cut off my prayer when I saw the still form of Raul, one of our missionaries and a pilot with the ministry. I walked over to where he lay on the body of the aircraft. "Osito," I said, calling the precious

Guatemalan man by his nickname ("Little Bear" in English because of his full black beard).

He didn't answer.

Osito had been full of life. He loved to joke and always laughed at his own jokes. Now he was gone from us, in the presence of the Lord.

I cannot explain what went on inside me. My prayer changed to, *Lord, this can't be!*

Stumbling in the mud, I trudged to the front of the aircraft's shell. I saw plane parts scattered all over the mountain and bodies covered with cloths. I asked J. D., the former missionary who came with me, to lift the cloth covering the nearest body.

Soon I looked on the face of my precious son-in-law Chris. He was already with the Lord. I choked back tears that demanded to fall. I asked J. D. to take the ring off his finger so I could give it to my daughter Kimberly. Fear, dread, and pain filled my being as I wondered who else lay beneath the makeshift shrouds.

My dear friend Pastor Chuck, whom I have known for more than forty years, stood over a couple of other bodies. I asked him if they were my husband or son.

"They're covered with so much mud, it's hard to tell."

I later learned these bodies were my husband Jim and son Jimmy. Chuck did not want to tell me. Because I didn't see them, I could believe they were still alive.

In denial, I quickly walked back down the mountain, slipping and sliding in mud, the guard holding onto my arm. I needed to get to the local general hospital as fast as I could. I had been told that some survivors from the plane had been taken there.

If I had slowed my pace, I would have heard my Father God speaking to my heart, telling me that neither my husband nor my son had survived. But at that time, I refused to believe it because my eyes had seen no proof.

At the hospital, I saw several group members who had worked at the campaign. I thanked the Lord that they were alive. None of them had serious injuries but rather bruises and emotional trauma. I dashed from person to person, asking, "Have you seen Jim or Jimmy?"

None had. I sat in a hospital room with another missionary, Marcia, and a friend, Anita Gonzales, from our church. I had so much anguish in my heart while waiting to hear some news. I silently prayed, repeatedly, *Lord, please let them be alive, or at least one of them.*

Hours passed, and finally Anita's husband, Dr. Gonzalez, gently touched my shoulder. Looking at his face, I knew he had words I did not want to hear.

"Neither of them made it," he said.

Finally, I let my ears hear what I already knew in my heart: my dear husband and son had gone to be with Jesus.

I cannot put my devastation into words. There is no way to explain it. I felt drained—an emotional wreck. Fear tried to rise in my heart at the thought that two of the people I loved most in the world were gone from my life. I would never again hear Jim's voice of love. I would never again hear my son say, "Mom."

Marcia and Anita walked me out of the hospital, one on each side holding me up. I was numb from head to toe, no life left in me. In those moments, I had no reason to keep on living. I had no understanding as to why this had happened. I wanted to go to bed and not wake up.

After arriving back on our Living Water Teaching campus, I went straight to my daughter-in-law's house. After hearing the comments as she climbed the hill, Laura had decided to not go to the accident site. I held Jimmy III, Alexis, and Jordan tightly. Laura had already accepted what I could not—that they were gone. Looking into her face, I saw grief, fear, anxiety, unanswered questions, and so much more. Her precious husband was gone, and their children would never see their daddy again this side of heaven.

A couple of the group members—friends she had known for some time—were with her. I did not know what to say to her since I was overcome with grief myself. I walked the short distance home.

I never knew such pain existed. A big, black hole filled my being. My mouth was full of gall. I could not eat. Marcia, a special friend and missionary, spent that Sunday night with me. I barely slept. I couldn't even pray or read my Bible with any understanding. I did not blame God. I have never blamed Him. This accident was not His doing. But it was an accident I could not explain.

The next day, our youngest daughter, Debbie, called. Her husband, Keith, who had been on the trip, was now back with her, but she wanted to hear her mama's voice. Her daddy, whom she loved, and her older brother were now gone from her life, and she was full of grief. As I talked with her through tears, I could hear her heart was broken into a thousand pieces. Her thoughts raced in circles as she wondered how we could face the future without those we loved so much.

My oldest daughter, Kimberly (whose husband Chris was also on the plane), called me from the States to confirm the awful news. She didn't want to believe it until she heard it from me. Not only was her husband gone but also her dad and brother. With her heart torn in shreds and through tear-filled words, she asked, "Mom, what are we going to do?"

She had three children: Christopher, ten; Matthew, seven; and Lynsey, four. They could never again on this earth talk with their dad, grandpa, or Uncle Jimmy.

I replied with all the faith I could muster, "We are going on."

I called my sister, Linda, in Kentucky to share the devastating news. She was in total shock. I asked her to go to Caddo Mills, Texas, to be with Kimberly and the children and to call my two brothers and let them know about the accident.

The next day was a blur. Several people from the ministry worked hard on the paperwork needed to send the bodies back to the United States. My heart went out to the group members who were returning without their mates. One precious father had to return without his son and four women without their husbands. I didn't know these group members very well. This was their first time on a mission trip with Living Water Teaching, and with 105 staff and volunteers on this trip, I didn't get to know them personally. I did call some of them a few days later to express my heartfelt sympathy, but what can you say at a time like this that will ease their pain? Only Jesus can do that!

It was devastation in mountain measure. Buckets of tears were shed. Hearts were torn apart. Thoughts dashed in and out. Numbness. Pain. Grief. Sadness. Swollen eyes. Fogginess. Eighteen people were on board. Eleven died— ten men and one woman. God spared seven lives. Those now in heaven included my husband Jim; our son, Jimmy; son-in-law Chris; two precious missionaries, Tom VanderPol and Raul Jacobs;

and six group members. Unbelievably, thirteen children within our ministry had been left without their daddies.

When Renae, Tom VanderPol's wife, heard the news of the crash and that her beloved husband had died, along with several others, she did not want to accept this truth. She had just seen him a few hours before, and now he was with the Lord. This was so hard for her to grasp. She had to face the future without the man that she truly loved. He wouldn't have the opportunity to even see his second baby.

Tom was only twenty-eight years old. He was a kind, gentle man with a sweet spirit. He was a great missionary, pilot, and mechanic. His walk with the Lord was evident in the way he lived his life. Tom loved the Lord, and his wife and family meant everything to him.

The remaining missionaries and staff finally arrived back at our Living Water campus Monday afternoon after two days of fighting vicious rain, mud, weariness, and lack of sleep. It had taken them fifty-eight hours. The weather was some of the worst they'd ever seen. The road through the mountains between Playa Grande and Coban was under construction and had many areas of deep mud. Several times they had to push the vehicles through the mud. Part of the road sunk down the mountain after the last vehicle passed. They arrived in Coban in the afternoon and discovered that a bridge they needed to cross was completely submerged in water, and the road was blocked by a landslide a few miles ahead. The team got a hotel and spent the night.

They'd planned to leave at around four o'clock Sunday morning, but they waited until eight to see if weather conditions would improve. As they left Coban, water came up over the tires. While traveling toward home, they encountered half a mountain that had collapsed and covered five hundred feet of the road. They had to wait in a line of vehicles for thirteen hours while workers cleared a path through the landslide.

While they waited, one of the women from our church found them and told them about the crash. Her family in Xela had called her with the news. The team listened to the radio in disbelief trying to piece together more details. They had no idea who was alive or who had died. Dr. Eckstein, a member of the US group, got out and slogged through the mud and over the landslide, trying to get to Xela and care for the injured.

Around nine in the evening, the road finally opened enough for them to drive through, but fallen rocks and stones flattened some tires. Hungry and wet, the team continued on to Guatemala City, arrived at a gas station around three in the morning, and rested in the vehicles for two hours. Then they got the flat tires fixed and drove to the Xela campus, arriving in the early afternoon.

Pastor Dan, Pastor Chuck, and other pastors met them as they arrived on campus and had them come to the dining hall to give them the details, pray for them, and comfort them. They also filled them in on the plans for the evening memorial service.

My son-in-law Keith had also been on the trip and experienced the same hazardous conditions. He drove separately with another missionary, a staff member, and several doctors so they could immediately fly back to the US after the campaign. But they encountered a mudslide that completely covered the main road. They had to abandon their vehicle. Carrying their luggage, they climbed the mudslide to get to the other side. The following morning, they rented a vehicle to take them to the city. Upon arriving at the hotel in Guatemala City, Keith received a call and learned that the plane had crashed and that his father-in-law and two brothers-in-law had died, along with several other people. He came back to the campus in Xela instead of going home.

The night after the accident, a Monday, we held a memorial service in our local church. The sanctuary was filled. Local pastors, church members, missionaries, staff, friends, volunteers from the US group, and lots of others had come to honor the lives of those who had died in the plane crash. The pastor had a good message. I thanked the people who came to show their love and respect, and I said a few words to honor the lives of those who had died. The service was beautiful. The funeral home was able to prepare only three of the bodies for the Monday night service: my husband Jim, our son Jimmy, and Raul Jacobs.

Raul's wife, Miriam, a missionary with us and our pharmacy overseer, was also on the trip but had returned to Xela on one of the three earlier flights. Raul's three teenage children were devastated when they heard that their father had died in the crash. Many family members and friends were present to say goodbye to someone who had brought great joy into their lives. Raul, a Guatemalan who spoke excellent English, was my husband's right arm, his interpreter on many occasions, traveling partner, good friend, and a precious missionary with Living Water Teaching. We all loved him.

On Tuesday morning, I told the missionaries and all our Guatemalan staff that Living Water Teaching would continue. It was a statement of faith. I recognized that the shoes I was stepping into were too big for me, but I also knew I was not going to let the devil win. I could have left the mission field and returned to the United States. No one would have questioned my decision. We had given nineteen years of our lives to the calling the Lord had put inside us. However, I knew in my heart that what the Lord called us to do in 1979 was not completed. As unbelievable as it may sound, I did not want to leave. I loved these people, and I still do. The Guatemalan people have become my people. Many of them are closer than my own family. I made the decision standing on faith that we would not quit.

On Tuesday afternoon, the remaining group members, my daughter-in-law, Laura, her three children, and I traveled to Guatemala City. There, the American Embassy gathered us all in one room to express their sorrow as well as their gratitude for all the group had done in the few short days of the medical campaign. They presented each family with a medal—the Quetzal of Peace. The next morning, we all flew back to the United States to accompany the bodies of our loved ones.

We were met by family when we arrived in Dallas: my two daughters, Kimberly and Debbie; my son-in-law Keith; my sister, Linda; and my two brothers, Joe and Jimmy, and their wives. They did not have to say anything. Just their presence meant everything to me.

3

REMINISCING ABOUT THAT FATAL DAY

It was the worst day of my life.

On Sunday, November 1, 1998, as I was getting ready to leave for church, my husband Jim called me to see how the weather was in Xela. It was good to hear his voice. Like me, he was excited that he would come home shortly. I told him that at the moment the sun was shining. We were both happy about that since sunshine made it easier to land on the dirt strip at the airport. We hung up the phone, thinking we would see each other later that day. I don't remember hearing anxiety in his voice, and he hadn't spoken of a premonition that they wouldn't arrive safely.

While sitting inside the church during the service, I heard a plane and thought, *Jim is home. He'll walk in the church door in just a short while.*

He never came.

I later learned that the plane I had heard was the third flight. Raul's wife, Miriam, was a passenger, as were many more group members from the US.

Eighteen people were left in Playa Grande, which included the two pilots. That would be the fourth and final trip out. Raul called Laura, my daughter-in-law, to check on the weather before they left. She told him there were still some openings in the sky. However, at an altitude of 7,800 feet, the sky could close at any minute.

Later, one of the survivors told me that those remaining in Playa Grande were anxious to leave the campaign site because the creek was rising, and the rain still poured down. They flew over Xela but could not find the runway because everything was socked in. They could not see a break in the clouds, so they flew back to Guatemala City but were not given permission to land at the airport, even though they had filed a flight plan.

Again, they returned to Xela and circled around until they found a small opening in the clouds. They descended through the clouds but came out on top of a mountain. A tall tree stood near the left engine. The branches grabbed the engine and broke it off the plane. The aircraft then crashed into the mountain.

I've tried to imagine what they went through in those last few moments before impact. Did they know the plane was going to crash? What were their last thoughts? Did they pray—call out to God? Did their lives pass before them?

I've also tried to imagine what Tom and my son went through trying to land the plane, hitting the trees, fighting with the yoke. Looking at each other, fear and terror on their faces, Jimmy hearing instructions from his dad and knowing eighteen precious people were on board. I have to believe God snatched them out of their bodies and took them immediately into His presence before they could hit the mountain and suffer agonizing pain.

It was an accident. No one was to blame, and no negligence was involved. No legal action was taken against the ministry. But what if they'd had permission to land in Guatemala City? What if they'd left Playa Grande earlier? What if . . . what if . . . ?

I don't know how to explain the accident. The campaign was a total success. God could have been trying to send some kind of a warning to the pilots, but in their rush to leave, they didn't sense any danger ahead. What I do know is that over a thousand people made the decision to move out of the kingdom of darkness and into the kingdom of light during that campaign. Many were healed, ministered to, and received the meds they needed. I know the devil was mad, and I know John 10:10 KJV says, "The thief cometh not, but for to steal, and to kill, and to destroy." Satan would like to take out anyone who is doing something for God. In that same verse, Jesus says, "I am come that they might have life, and that they might have it more abundantly."

4

ALiVE AND GiViNG GOD PRAiSE

One of the survivors of the accident, a young girl named Sunshine, told me her testimony about the crash. A Native American, Sunshine had made several trips to Guatemala with her youth group from Corona, California, since she was thirteen. She was now eighteen.

This time she flew into Guatemala City along with other group members, including doctors and other medical personnel, for the campaign in Playa Grande.

This is Sunshine's testimony:

> The following morning, Pastor Jim and Marion met up with our group to fly in with us to Playa Grande. The ministry's DC-3 would take half of the group, and a military DC-3 would take the rest. I was excited to fly in the

military plane because it was not like a normal airplane with rows of seats spanning the aircraft's interior. This plane had just one row of seats on each side of the plane from back to front. I met a twenty-one-year-old man from Indiana, Ross, who was making his first trip to Guatemala with Living Water Teaching.

When both aircraft arrived in Playa Grande, we rode in the back of what looked like cattle trucks to the campaign site. We crossed a bridge over a large body of water, which caused me to panic because the bridge was so narrow and the trucks so heavy.

At the campaign site, people stood in line as far as we could see. We unloaded and got our bunking assignments, separating the women from the men. After we put away our belongings, each person received their instructions for the campaign. I would be a runner, along with Ross, the rookie from Indiana. We had many doctors on this trip, so we both were to be runners to get anything they needed or to cover other staff members' breaks.

This was the biggest medical and dental campaign I had ever seen. Over the three days of clinic, the lines never seemed to get smaller. People kept coming and coming. I also saw more people coming to salvation on this campaign than at any other.

The afternoon of the third and last day of the clinic, we packed our things and headed by groups to the airfield to fly to Xela. I was in the last group because they needed to get the doctors and some of the other team members on the first flight out. Marion left on the second flight out, and Pastor Jim stayed with my group. The missionaries and staff left at daylight Saturday morning.

When only two groups remained, the weather turned bad. The wind was crazy, and rain fell hard. That night we all slept on tables in one big room together because the electricity had gone out. Pastor Jim shared a word with us that night, quoting a book he was writing about Naomi and Ruth. He said that when God put a ministry together, no one or nothing could stop it. If something happened to him, he said, the ministry would continue through his wife, Marion, because God had birthed the ministry in both of them. As with Ruth and Naomi, the ministry would go on because of God's faithfulness and His calling on the ministry of Living Water Teaching. He also said that if anything happened to him, he wanted Marion to marry again. This would prove they'd had a happy marriage. (Marion said that she had heard this same thing now from two different people on this ministry team and was wondering if God was trying to say something to Jim.)

The next morning, we woke up and packed all the luggage into the back of three trucks, and the remaining group members climbed in. Trees had blown down all around us, and the road had turned to mud. When we got to the airfield, the ministry plane had not yet arrived, so we unloaded all the luggage from the trucks and had a snack. A few minutes later, Jimmy landed and talked with his dad about the hurricane. They agreed that they had enough time to fly the next group to Xela and return for the few of us who would stay behind with the luggage. Tom took the pilot's seat with Jimmy as copilot.

The third group left Playa Grande on Sunday morning and arrived in Xela around eleven. After they unloaded the plane, they headed back to Playa Grande to pick up the remaining sixteen people, making a total of eighteen, including the pilots.

As soon as the plane landed, we stacked the luggage in the cargo area. Jim assigned seats based on the passengers' age and weight. He put Ross, the young man, beside me on the plane. Again, Tom was the pilot, Jimmy was the copilot, and Chris, Jim's son-in-law, took the jump seat.

I fell asleep and woke up later to Jim and Raul walking around in the plane and speaking very fast in Spanish. I could tell something was wrong. When I looked out the window, it was dark with dense fog and hard rain.

Again, I fell asleep, but this time I awakened with a jolt. The plane's nose was pitching up fast. All I could see was a mountain.

Then I heard a terrible scream. I looked at Ross, then the plane hit something. The lights went out, but we were still going. It hit something else. Everything went black.

When I came to, I was dizzy. I could barely breathe, and I could not move. I kept passing out, and when I opened my eyes again, I could see two ladies passed out in front of me on the floor while others prayed.

I felt paralyzed with feelings of pins and needles pricking my entire body. Then someone directly behind me touched my back.

It was Ross. He couldn't talk and wasn't breathing right. I kept passing out, and when I came to again, one of the ladies was missing from the floor. I passed out again and then opened my eyes, and the second lady was gone. I prayed but didn't know if I was praying to live or to die.

People around me were speaking Spanish. Over and over, I cried out for help. It was getting harder to breathe because people were stepping on us, opening our suitcases, and taking what they wanted. These were local people that arrived before the military and were never found out. I looked around again to see a guy coming toward me, swinging a machete. I tried to scream for him to stop. My mouth was so dry.

He kept swinging and hitting whatever I was stuck in. I saw people being taken out on stretchers. I kept saying, "Ross, are you okay? Keep breathing!"

He grabbed my hand, and I realized I was not paralyzed because I could feel his grip, but I knew he was not okay. I passed out again, and then as I opened my eyes, I could finally take in a full breath of air. A man was pulling me up by my arms.

Soon I discovered Ross and I had been wrapped up together with rows of seats around us, luggage piled on top of us and behind us. When I looked around at the magnitude of the situation, I felt overwhelmed with sadness and loss. Nothing about this wreckage remotely resembled Mercy Wings, the ministry airplane. Most of it was gone.

"I have to go and get help," I said to Ross. "I'll be back for you. I promise."

He was scared. I could tell. I tried to walk, but it hurt, and I fell to the ground. As a man helped me up, I saw others dragging Ross behind me on a stretcher.

We needed help fast to be able to get back to the mission and tell Marion that the plane had crashed. I ran down the muddy mountain about a hundred and twenty-five feet as quickly as I could. I kept falling and getting back up. Then I saw three men in a truck. They spoke only Spanish, so I waved toward the plane. They helped me in the back of the truck, and we drove back up to the crash site. I led one of them to Ross, and they put him in the back of the truck. I rode in front with the other two guys.

I knew that no one on the campus had heard about the crash. I had not seen Jim, Jimmy, Tom, Raul, nor Chris. Other than them, no one on the plane had ever been to Guatemala, let alone the campus. I kept telling the men that Living Water Teaching was close to the zoo, but they did not understand. So I began making animal noises, and then they understood.

I then passed out. When I awakened, we had parked in front of the zoo. I directed them to the campus. The guard at the gate recognized me, and his eyes betrayed his concern. No doubt, he wondered what these men had done to me and why was I in this truck with them. I just kept saying, "The plane crashed, and Ross cannot breathe."

They asked, "Where is Pastor Jim, Jimmy, Raul, Tom?"

I didn't know. I started crying and shaking my head, feeling as if I was losing it. I cried out, "Get Marion. Call Dany."

I woke up in a shower in one of the bungalows on the Bible school campus as some of the women from the US group were trying to wake me up to see what happened. I screamed because they were washing my hair, and it felt as if they were cutting my scalp. They could not understand why I had so much metal in my hair. They had not yet heard that the plane had crashed. I was covered with jet fuel, and that was why I kept passing out.

The next time I came to, I was lying in a bed in my room in the bungalow on campus. Carol, one of the missionaries, asked me if I was okay. I said, "I can't move my neck, and my whole body hurts."

I started crying. They took me to the hospital, and I was released shortly thereafter because I had no serious in-juries. Ross was banged up pretty bad but had no broken bones, just lots of bruises. The other five surviving mem-bers of the US group were taken to the hospital, treated and released and were able to return home on their original flights two days later.

I stayed in contact with Sunshine by email. By the time she went home, she was fully healed of any injuries. After two months, she was healed emotion-ally of her nightmares. She said, "I have no mental or physical trauma. God has done a miracle in my life."

All praise goes to God!

5

HONORING GOD'S CHAMPIONS

I t is never easy to say goodbye to those you love.

I knew the next couple of days would be filled with making arrangements for the service, calling the people we wanted to participate, picking out the coffins and burial plots, writing the announcement for the paper, etc. Thank God for His grace and help in getting it all done.

I called Pastor Butch Bruton at New Life Family Fellowship, where we attended church in Caddo Mills. I asked to have the home-going service there for Jim, Jimmy, and Chris. He answered that we could.

Brother Copeland of Kenneth Copeland Ministries, a friend and financial supporter of Living Water Teaching, called me and offered his help. I asked him to minister the Word during the service. I asked Jim's very close friend, Pastor Sherman Owens, to emcee the service, and his daughter, Mary Beth, agreed to sing. After Pastor Sherman opened the service, we sang two congregational songs, and Mary Beth sang. Jim's brother, Reverend Jerry Zirkle, shared a word of encouragement and his love for his brother, along with several other pastors and friends that spoke encouraging words.

And then Brother Copeland ministered the Word. After the message, he gave an altar call. The mother of my son-in-law Keith gave her heart to the Lord.

I spoke for a few minutes, sharing my appreciation to all those who had come, and I wanted all to know that the ministry of Living Water Teaching would continue. Pastor Sherman told some funny little stories about his friendship with Jim, and he then shared some Scriptures. The church was packed with family members and friends. The service lasted three and a half hours. It was too dark to go to the cemetery afterward, so they were buried early the next morning.

News of the crash spread rapidly from state to state and even into other countries. Jim was a visionary and had traveled extensively throughout the United States. We had just returned from a trip to Germany and Sweden, where he shared the Word of God and spoke about the work in Central America. One month later, he was with Jesus.

6

THE AFTERMATH

I never knew such pain existed.

The days and weeks following the accident were some of the darkest and toughest days of my life. I felt as if I were in limbo.

I slept at my daughter-in-law's home. As a widow, she would now have to raise her three little ones by herself. Jimmy was her life, and she now had to explain to her three babies where their father was.

I could not stand the thought of sleeping in my big house by myself, so every night, I walked the dozen or so yards to Laura's house at bedtime and spent the night. And every morning for at least two weeks, the moment I opened my eyes, the Enemy was in my face, harassing me.

What are you going to do now? You are not a leader.

I came right back at him with the Word of God. I declared out loud, "I am more than a conqueror through Him who loved me. I can do all things through Christ who strengthens me."

That was my spirit talking, but my flesh cried out, *Lord, I can't do this! It's too overwhelming. It's bigger than I am.*

Thank the Lord for the body of Christ. Their prayers carried me, sustained me, encouraged me, and upheld me. Only God's grace enabled me to put one foot in front of the other. I cannot count how many times I wanted to throw in the towel, but as the Word declares in James 4:6, "He gives more grace."

Two months after the accident, I still struggled. I tried to pray, but tears came like a gusher. Several times I screamed at the devil, "You are a loser! I am a winner, and this ministry is going to continue by the grace of God!" I got angry and my emotions were out of control as I cried out to the Lord, *Lord, why didn't I die in that accident? It hurts! The pain is unbearable! Holy Spirit, help me.*

I began opening my heart completely to Jesus, who is the healer, asking Him to heal my emotions and take away the pain. At the same time, great sobs came from down deep in my innermost being, and I would give into that until I felt a release, and then I would continue to just worship. I would sit quietly in His presence and let His peace fill my heart. I would thank Him for His healing power. I would thank Him that I didn't die in the crash. I would thank Him that the ministry would continue, and I would thank Him for the privilege to be alive for my family.

This happened time and again during the first few months. I would hear an airplane and think, *Jim and Jimmy are back.* I would walk into a room and believe that Jim would be sitting there. I needed healing in my emotions. My healing didn't come all at once but over a period of time as I went often to my secret place (my place of prayer).

Laura, my daughter-in-law, her three children, and I decided to stay in the States for the Christmas holidays. I knew that being around family with my two daughters and their children would bring joy and some type of healing into our hearts.

In January, two months after the accident, I went to a ministers' conference in the States. I needed to hear from God. I needed my strength renewed. I needed peace of mind. I needed emotional healing. I just wanted to sit and take in the Word of God, to take in Jesus, who is the Word. During one of the night services, Brother Copeland stepped down off the platform and came to me.

He looked me right in the eye and said, "This ministry is going to grow far greater—far greater—than it did prior to Jim's home-going. The best is yet to come. The flow has only begun. Things look one way, but they are going another way in the Spirit. Very shortly, things in the natural will make a turn and line up with the Spirit, for things have already been put into motion. The roots are deep, and failure is not even an option, saith the Lord."

Brother Copeland continued with the prophecy, saying, "The voice of the Lord came to me saying, 'I, the Lord, talked to your husband about this. I visited with him about it, and your husband said it was well and good for the Holy Ghost to anoint you and double for your shame.' The only thing your husband said was to tell her to rest. So the Lord said, 'I am telling you to rest. That's what your husband Jim said he is supposed to tell you. So rest! Hard work ain't going to do it anyhow. Faith is what is going to do it. We will go with you. Yes and amen, hallelujah!' "

You cannot imagine the encouragement this brought. I began to talk to the Lord, saying, *Lord, this vision didn't die with Jim. It is my vision also. I am not the leader Jim was, but I don't have to be. I will lead, leaning heavily on You, Lord. I accept what Brother Copeland said to me. This ministry is yours, Lord Jesus. This vision came directly from the throne of grace. I refuse to let Jim, Jimmy, Chris, Tom, and Raul's work die.*

After the accident, I learned the power of praise. I grew in my leadership abilities. I began to develop self-confidence. I kept good, encouraging people around me. Just knowing my family, the missionaries, our local church, and the staff were all with me gave me great boldness to take it one day at a time.

It did not happen overnight, nor in a few weeks or months, but about two years later, I could think of them without a dam breaking loose. I'm not saying tears never filled my eyes again, but the pain, the loss, the missing them got easier. I had Bible school classes to teach, medical campaigns to help set up, youth trips to attend, and fundraising trips to take. My life was busy and becoming productive again. I knew Jim would want the ministry to continue and would not want me to live in grief.

I don't know how people without God, without His Word, can face tragedies like this—or something similar—and triumph. The sad thing is many do not. Some turn to alcohol and drugs. Others give up and even lose their mind. Many people commit suicide. But I know that if a person has Jesus Christ, the healer, the sustainer, the one who is more than enough, they can come through any tragedy, affliction, death, or illness and triumph.

The devil rocked my boat, but he didn't sink it. He knocked me over but not out.

I learned to tap into the grace of God. I had to rely on His grace to give me the strength to stand firm when I felt inadequate being out in front of the ministry. His grace helped me to do that. His grace was present when doubt and fear tried to invade my mind. I would say, "Lord, Your grace is sufficient to bring me through this." I knew that I could not do anything without the help of the Lord, but with Him, I believed

I could do all things. I could minister the Word in churches, I could raise funds for the ministry stateside, have a staff meeting, make the right decisions concerning the ministry or whatever was needed to be done in the leadership position. When thoughts would come to me like, "You don't have the ability to do this," or, "You are not a leader," I would say, "With God, I can do all things." It was His grace that enabled me to put one foot in front of the other and continue the vision of Living Water Teaching. Grace is many things. It is God's ability in us to do what we cannot do on our own. It is His enabling power in us to stand, regardless of any attack of the Enemy. Grace is also God's unmerited favor; it is a never-ending flow of power. Grace is a gift from God. He tells us in Ephesians 2:8, "For by grace, you have been saved through faith, and that not of yourselves; it is the gift of God." We can do nothing to earn, work for, or deserve God's salvation, redemption, forgiveness, blessing, or acceptance. He declares that we are without guilt, and He calls us His own. Grace is always based on God, not on us. He initiated it, provided it, and paid for it.

The basis of grace is God's love for us. Our relationship with God is not based on our performance as good Christians. It's based on the Father's love, which brings about our well-being. I know God loves me. We can do nothing to make God stop loving us. His nature is to love. That is who He is!

7

FULL SPEED AHEAD

The best is yet to come! Thank God that we had a strong staff and well-trained people in place at the time of the accident. Jim had weekly staff meetings, and during those times, he openly handled any problems or conflicts. After a campaign, we always evaluated the things we did right and opened a discussion about things we could have done better. Jim was a strong leader with a strong personality and constantly trained staff and missionaries. He didn't tiptoe around issues but was direct and to the point, letting his staff know how he wanted things done. I walked by Jim's side and learned how to handle things as he would.

All the missionaries knew their place within the ministry and trained those who worked under them in the areas of construction, maintenance, kitchen, school, trips, Bible school classes, etc. Most of our missionaries came out of a Bible school or a church that preached the truth of the Word.

If they believed God had called them to work with Living Water Teaching, they had to come on a qualifying trip to the field and have an interview with the director. They then returned for thirty days of orientation, visiting every department of the ministry, listening to teachings of missionaries about things they had learned, hearing Jim's teachings, and reading each of his books on missions.

Then the acceptance committee made their decision. If they offered a position, the new missionaries went home and raised the required funds before returning to the field. (In order to work with us, our missionaries must be debt free.) They then signed a two- or four-year contract. We wanted missionaries who believed they had a call and not just a burden.

In Jim's book *The Burden or the Call*, he explained that visiting the mission field is the best way for people to learn whether they have a burden or a call. Imagine that two people come on the same trip and experience the same difficulties. For example, half of the time, they have no electricity. Water is rationed, so they can't take a shower every day. They don't recognize some of the food on their plates. They have to drop their used toilet tissue into a basket beside the commode. The nights are short and the days are long. They wearily crawl into their sleeping bag and discover a bed partner with more than six legs.

They lie awake, thinking about the next day when they'll work in the medical clinic. "I get to pray for the sick," they say. The next day, they lay hands on them for prayer, turning their heads because of bad breath and unwashed bodies. But they can't have a conversation because they can't speak the language, so they need an interpreter.

When the ten days are over, the one with the burden says, *Thank You, Lord, for Brother Jim. I'm so glad You sent him to Guatemala. I'm going to pray for him every day and send him financial support every month, but please do not ever send me back to that place again.*

The one with the call says, *Father God, let me go back to Guatemala. Let me lay hands on the sick. Let me wipe noses, change diapers, and kiss bruises because that is what ministry is all about. Send me!*

Our local church was pastored by a Guatemalan, a graduate of our Bible school. He spoke good English and was a missionary with us. After the accident, my greatest cheerleader was our Bible school director, Carol Schlimmer. She had been a missionary with us for about seventeen years at the time of the accident. Many times, she told me, "You can do this. You are God's anointed leader now." She walked by my side, she encouraged me, and she also helped to oversee the ministry until I could take the reins.

I knew we needed another director over the

ministry because Carol already worked full-time at the Bible school. I needed to learn from someone who had more experience than I did. A short time later, a former missionary, Dr. Paul Burge, and his wife, Betty, who were serving in Sweden at the time, graciously returned to help until I could gain the knowledge and confidence I needed to lead the ministry. I walked by Jim's side but never in his shoes. I knew my place in the ministry, but to be out in front leading in my emotional state, I felt like I needed more time. Dr. Paul filled in for two years as director, and he worked very closely with me until I felt that I could stand on my own two feet as president.

The hardest thing for me after the accident was going to the US to raise funds for the ministry. Jim was so good at it. He was a natural at fundraising, but I was not. Our expenses included monthly salaries for around forty people in Guatemala and eight in the US, upkeep on thirty-six buildings, electricity, gas, repairs, vehicle maintenance, etc. Our donors helped every month, but not enough came in to take care of all we were doing.

The accident occurred on November 1, 1998, and I took my first fundraising trip to the US by myself in April 1999. The US office had contacted some of our supporting churches, and they wanted me to come. I had a message prepared, but it was hard for me to get through it without tears. Traveling by myself was not a good idea. I felt lonely in hotels. When I stayed by myself, the thoughts always came and then the tears.

During my next trip out, I took another missionary woman with me. She spoke at some of the churches, and I spoke at others. On another occasion, I took my daughter along. Soon I grew in confidence that I, too, could be an effective fundraiser.

8

A COUNTRY GIRL

I never thought I would leave Kentucky, but God had a plan for my life that would take me to many parts of the world.

I was born in Springfield, Kentucky, which is a small city about sixty miles from Louisville. When I was a few months old, we moved to Willisburg and stayed there until I was eight. My daddy's name is Clarence, and he was a farmer. Our family raised tobacco on our 108-acre farm. We grew our own vegetables and had chickens and a smokehouse where my Grandpa Kays cured hams. A cistern was our water source. We didn't have a water pump, but Daddy used a bucket to draw water from the well. We also had a cellar where my mom, Jane, stored her canned fruits and vegetables. We did not have running water or an indoor bathroom. Instead, we had a hen house, which we visited many times a day because Daddy never built an outhouse.

Our house was heated by a wood stove, which Mama also used to heat the iron to press our clothing. Kerosene lamps lit our home at night. Since we had no indoor plumbing, Mama had to heat water in a big, galvanized tub for our baths. The dirtiest of the three of us children went last because we used the same water.

Mama dried our clean laundry on a clothesline. She once told me that she didn't have baby seats or chairs to put Linda and me in while she went outside to hang up clothes. Instead, she always sat us down beside a bedpost, raised the edge of the bed, and then lowered the post onto the hems of our dresses so we couldn't move until she came back in.

My older brother, Joe, is fourteen months older than I am. My sister, Linda, is two and a half years younger. We helped on the farm, with everyone doing their part in planting tobacco. My job was to pack the dirt around the tobacco plants after Daddy dropped them into a small hole. Then, when the tobacco was ready for harvesting, Daddy and Mama stripped it and put it in the barn to dry. We gathered eggs from the hen house, fed the chickens, picked blackberries, and did other little chores on the farm as necessary. We were poor, but as kids, we didn't know it. We always had plenty to eat.

Me and my siblings
in front of the tobacco fields

Joe and I had to walk about half a mile down a dirt road to catch the bus to take us to school. I was not quite five, and Linda was too young to begin classes. On our way, we often stopped to lick the cows' salt block. Occasionally, we missed the bus because we dawdled too much. Then we had to walk to our teacher's house close by and get a ride with her.

If I remember correctly, our school had two rooms. One of my favorite days was Valentine's Day, when all the kids exchanged valentines. I always took them home and read each one several times, relishing the fact that I had so many friends who loved me. That is what the valentines said.

I also remember my worst day. We had a tin slide on the playground, and I wanted to go down it. When I got to the top and touched the slide, it was scorching hot. I changed my mind, deciding I

didn't want to go down after all. But the kids behind me wouldn't let me back down the steps, so I
had to go down. I wanted to scream because it was
so hot. It took some skin off the backs of my legs
because I had a dress on. I was only five years old,
but I never forgot that.

We got one new pair of shoes each year. When
the soles of our shoes wore out, we put cardboard in
them to fill in the holes. We wore shoes to church
and school. Otherwise, we ran and played bare-
footed. Mama made Linda's and my dresses from
pretty feed-sack patterns that she picked out. The
sacks came full of corn. Joe got a lot of hand me
downs from his cousins.

We had fun on the farm, playing hide and seek,
red rover, kick the can, mother may I, and chase
and catch with our cousins. We rode horses and
laughed a lot. Linda and I played house on bales of
hay in the barn. We set up the bales to make walls,
and our house was in the middle of them. I always
told Linda, "You be the mom, and I'll be the baby,"
because the baby always got all the crackers. I did
that every time, but Linda was too young to understand. Sometimes she and I sat in the barn window
and sang as loud as we could.

I remember one day when we three kids got
into Daddy's car, and one of us moved the gear-
shift. We began rolling down the hill, hollering at

the top of our lungs for Daddy to come and save us. Joe and I got a taste of Daddy's belt. No one could accuse our parents of sparing the rod and spoiling the child.

We attended a small Baptist church in town where Linda and I sang in the children's choir. I don't remember too much else about the church, as I was quite small and that was over seventy years ago. But I do remember the little corner drug store where we got ice cream cones, and my, how that made our day. The town had just one main road. At the edge of town was the cemetery where many family members had been buried. We visited often, and on Memorial Day we met other family members, spread blankets on the ground, and had dinner together.

When I was eight years old, we moved from our tobacco farm in Willisburg, Kentucky, to the big city of Louisville. Joe, Linda, and I attended public schools and did well in our studies. When I was ten years old, Mama gave birth to a bouncing baby boy named Jimmy. A popular song at that time was titled "Bimbo," and Jimmy somehow acquired that nickname. He was Bimbo to all of us, and he was like my baby. I helped take care of him, changed his diapers, and gave him his bottles. Now, as a grown man, he is the biggest of us all.

Me and my siblings

I truly believe that the upbringing I had as a child— raised on a farm, poor but not really knowing it—prepared me for the mission field. I've been in places where there was no running water, no modern bathroom facilities, and at times no electricity, but I knew how to make the best of it. We did a medical campaign in a remote village for one week, and there was only one spicket in the whole town that had water. We didn't get a shower or wash our hair for a whole week. All of the women slept in one room on cots or sleeping bags on the floor as well as the men. We had an outside toilet in a little tiny building. We gladly did it because each day we had the privilege to attend to the medical needs of the people and had the opportunity to pray with them.

A child raised having everything that they ever wanted or needed, just handed to them, would be very difficult to almost impossible to make it on the mission field.

9

MY CALL

When I was fifteen years old, I knew God was calling me to be a missionary. I cannot explain exactly how I knew this, but I knew it in my heart. It was a dream God put there—a desire in my inner being. It was confirmed when I was seventeen and a missionary visited our church in Louisville, Kentucky. The woman was a Church of God missionary who had served in Africa for years.

I remember how my heart did flip-flops as she shared some of her experiences. I got excited and knew I would do some of the same things. At that moment, I didn't know where. I shared this news with my pastor, but I found no encouragement at the time. He told me many years later, "I thought you were just a young girl with a dream."

How right he was!

I dated several guys in my teenage years, but none with whom I wanted to spend the rest of my life. I had been praying for years that I would know and marry the right person because I had given my heart completely to the Lord and it was important whom I would marry. One day, when I was twenty years old and working as a secretary in a printing company, a handsome young man walked through my office.

The Spirit of God spoke to me, saying, *There goes your future husband.*

My gaze followed him through the office and out the door. He began working in the same building as I did but on a lower floor.

I continued to talk with the Lord because I needed to make sure I had heard Him correctly. I prayed, *If this is You, Lord, speak to him to ask me for a date.*

A few days later, on a Friday, he asked me out. We had a nice dinner and talked for about two hours. In our conversation, I did mention to him about my call to become a missionary. I wanted to be upfront with him from the beginning. If he had no interest in me after that, then so be it.

He made no comment. My words seemed to go in one ear and out the other. I did not push it, but I felt we would talk about it again. I knew the Lord could see our future when I could not, and I also knew the Lord had His hand upon Jim. I believed with all my heart that He had brought us together. Apparently, he liked what he saw and heard because he then asked me if I had plans for the next night. I had a ticket to attend a big gospel concert. My seat was originally near the front of the auditorium, but I wanted to sit with Jim, so I traded with someone and got two tickets way up in the balcony. The trade was worth it.

I invited Jim to our church the next morning. It was important to me to see if he would like my church and what I believed. If he didn't, our friendship would end right there. I was completely dedicated to the Lord, and it was vitally important to me that my husband and I walk together in agreement.

He said afterward, "I haven't felt this good in years."

Jim had recently returned from the Air Force in Greenland and had always attended a denominational church with his mom before enlisting. His father died when he was quite young, and his mother doted on him.

Our church had great music and a pastor who preached the Word with enthusiasm, and the people were happy and said "Amen." I attended this church for many years before I met Jim. I taught the junior Sunday school class, sang in the choir, and was part of a girl's quartet.

Jim liked the church. I continued to pray about our relationship and believed the Lord was giving me confirmation that Jim was the right one for me. Jim was a baby Christian, but as he continued faithfully in our church, I saw spiritual growth in his life. As far as the calling on my life, I knew Jim would someday be ready to hear and be a part of it, but the timing was not yet.

We continued growing in our relationship, getting to know each other. I had peace in my heart, and so did Jim. We talked about marriage a few times and believed God brought us together.

Jim proposed a short time later. I said, "yes", and we were married in our local church. I was one month from turning twenty-one.

Jim and me on our wedding day

10

THE BEGINNING
OF OUR FAMILY

We were married a little over a year when the Lord blessed us with a beautiful daughter, whom we named Kimberly Kay. When she was three months old, we moved to Jim's home state of Ohio, where he started a construction business. We found a small Church of God close to our home and began attending there. After several months, I became the young people's teacher. They were dear to my heart, and I loved the pastor and the people.

Jim attended but didn't seem to get as much out of it as I did. He did not attend every Sunday, but I always took the children. The Lord had blessed us with two more precious children: our son, Jimmy, and our baby daughter, Debbie.

Jim worked while I took care of the kids and made the house into a home. We were happy and growing in our marriage and as a family. I did not bring up the subject again of moving to the field and being a missionary, but I remember saying to the Lord, *I am going to put my call to missions on the back burner until you speak to Jim.*

I knew the timing was not right yet. When the Lord speaks to you about a calling, it does not necessarily mean it's going to happen in the next few weeks, months, or years. Neither Jim nor I were spiritually ready to leave for the mission field. I continued to bathe in prayer what the Lord had spoken to my heart and knew it would happen in the Lord's timing.

A few years passed, and our children grew. Early one morning, when Jimmy was four years old, he was playing with matches and set the kitchen trash on fire. Not knowing what to do, he got in bed with his big sister Kimberly.

I awoke to a loud crackling noise and opened our bedroom door. All I could see was smoke.

Jim had already gone to work, and nine-month-old Debbie was asleep in her bed in our room. All I could think of was getting my kids out.

I screamed, "Kimberly! Jimmy! Run!"

I grabbed Debbie and threw a blanket over her. I ran down the stairs as fast as I could and through the kitchen, flames shooting up through the ceiling, right into Jimmy's bedroom. Thank God he was in bed with his sister. The fire singed my hair as I ran through the house. We all went to the hospital for smoke inhalation but were released shortly thereafter.

Our home was gutted. The fire and the water hose ruined most of our furniture. We were able to salvage our clothing. Some of our furniture was saved, sanded, and revarnished. The police came, investigated, and determined that the fire was caused by faulty wiring. A few years later, when Jimmy was about nine years old, we were sitting at the dinner table one night, and he started talking about the fire.

He said, "Dad, Mom, remember the fire we had? I was playing with matches and set a piece of paper on fire. I accidentally dropped it into the wastebasket, where more paper caught fire, and then it just got bigger and I couldn't put it out."

My heart felt heavy because he had carried this inside him all that time. God had protected us. I knew He had a plan for our lives.

11

PREPARATION FOR OUR CALL

Preparation time is never wasted time.

Ohio was very cold, and often the snow covered the ground from November until March. Our children grew and started school. We still attended the Church of God down the road.

A young minister came to our church and began to teach some new things from *The Authority of the Believer*, by Reverend Kenneth Hagin. I had been the spiritual leader in our home for years. I prayed and asked the Lord to touch Jim and change his life completely and also asked that he would become our spiritual leader. Jim also heard some things from our new pastor that began to stir his heart.

He bought the same book and read and studied it. Jim soon changed right before my eyes. He began reading the Word of God with new passion. I wasn't sure exactly what was happening, but I truly liked it!

We had wonderful times of fellowship with the pastor and his wife and family. They shared so much truth from the Word of God with us and with the church, and we began to grow spiritually. We knew God had sent them there for the spiritual growth of the church and for our minds to be renewed in the Word of God.

Jim's work as a carpenter had basically come to a halt because of the very cold weather in Akron, Ohio. His cousin's husband invited him to come and work with him in Wheeling, West Virginia. It about broke my heart to leave the young people in my Sunday school class. I loved them like my own children. One of the young men in my class has now been a pastor for about thirty-five years and is doing great.

Looking back years later, we saw that the Lord was taking us on a long journey, getting us ready to go where He wanted us to be. Our West Virginia Church of God pastor knew of Brother Hagin and his Bible school in Broken Arrow, Oklahoma. We worked with this pastor for about a year and a half, teaching the Word of God to His people. Jim became the Sunday school superintendent and taught some in the men's prison. More importantly, we knew in our hearts that the Lord wanted us to attend Bible school because there was more He wanted us to do.

We both applied and were accepted. We packed up our home, sold our car, and all five of us rode in the front seat of a Ryder moving truck to Broken Arrow, Oklahoma.

As we pulled into the apartment complex where we would live, a couple waited for us. They had just graduated from Bible school, and the Lord had told them of a new family they needed to meet. We had some great times of fellowship with this couple. In one of our conversations, we learned that the wife had a niece who was a missionary in Guatemala. The Lord was at work behind the scenes.

We began our first classes at Rhema Bible Training Center in August 1977. The Word was rich, and we learned so much. It changed our lives and our way of thinking, solidified our marriage, and helped us to understand that we were sons and daughters of God. We were new creations in Christ Jesus, brought from death into life. Jesus was our Savior, our healer, our everything. God was a good God, He was our heavenly Father, and the Holy Spirit was a person who lived inside us to help us in our daily walk.

I knew a lot of these things already but had new understanding as our minds were renewed in the Word of God. Jim wanted to share what we were receiving with this missionary family in Guatemala. We began financially supporting this missionary family and sending letters, sharing about the things we were learning.

We attended Bible classes in the mornings. In the afternoons, Jim worked construction, and I watched a little girl for extra income.

Nick, the missionary from Guatemala, got excited about the teaching Jim was sending him, so he invited Jim to visit in February and to preach in several Guatemalan churches and share the Word of God. It so happened that Brother Hagin needed someone to take some books to Guatemala and give them to another missionary serving in Guatemala City. Guess who volunteered? Jim wanted to go but knew there was no way he could miss his classes or pay the airplane costs. We saw the hand of God move in this situation and open the door to where God was sending us, and the Bible school even covered the plane trip there and back. God was at work, and all Jim's expenses were covered.

The dean at Rhema gave Jim permission to take the books and spend ten days with the missionary family in Guatemala. Jim traveled to many different *pueblos* (towns) and preached the Word of God with the missionary serving as his interpreter. Jim returned home to Tulsa so elated that his time in Guatemala was all he could speak about for weeks.

Our three children were in school, so I took a job at the Howard Johnson motel to help pay the bills and buy food. I had fifteen rooms to clean daily if they were rented. Jim was in the second year at Rhema, and he continued working construction in the afternoons. I attended only one year and then graduated, but I attended all the special meetings with him.

After Jim graduated in May, he said, "Marion, I want you to take a trip with me to Guatemala. We'll take several others and make it a mission trip." So, in June of 1979, a small group of fifteen accompanied us to Guatemala, including Jim's sister, his nephew, their pastor and his wife from Ohio, other members from that church, and my former student, who is now a pastor in Colorado.

I remember saying to the Lord, *If you want us to move to Guatemala and if this is the call you put in my heart many years back, please confirm it to me on this trip.*

The Lord had already spoken to Jim's heart. He knew we were supposed to begin a work in Guatemala, and he was thinking of ways to convince me.

We visited and ministered to tribes of indigenous Indians in several different pueblos. The women came in their typical colorful clothing with skirts (*cortes*) that identified their tribe and beautiful blouses (*guipils*), and the men dressed in ordinary pants and shirts. The men sat on one side of the church and the women on the other side. They made joyful noises unto the Lord with four or five members leading the song service. They seemed like happy people. We each had our turn ministering the Word with an interpreter in all the villages we visited. I also sang the one song I'd learned in Spanish: "Por Su Palabra" ("By His Word").

I saw poverty. I saw the primitive way many families lived with no indoor plumbing. The people cooked on an open fire and slept on a floor mat or bed of straw. They bargained in the open market. They washed their clothing on a *pila* (a washboard made of either plastic or cement) and then spread their clothing on bushes or the ground to dry. Their way of living was foreign to me.

I thought, *Lord, how will my children adjust to this culture? How will I?*

Deep inside, I knew the Lord wanted us in Guatemala. We had something these precious people needed: not religion—Jesus. I walked the land and prayed, and so did Jim. The Lord was talking to both of us, confirming His calling on our lives. We knew our children would not think moving to Guatemala was good news, but it was settled in our hearts.

I stand amazed at the goodness of God. He had spoken to my heart about missions when I was fifteen. Now I was thirty-four and moving to the mission field. I didn't have to convince Jim because the Lord had it all planned out. We now had something to say, teach, preach, and show by example.

We returned home to Tulsa. That first night while eating supper together, we began to share with the kids what the Lord had spoken to us.

Shock and tears followed first with Kimberly, age thirteen. "Go ahead, Daddy," she said. "I'm going to stay with Uncle Jerry." (Jerry was Jim's brother.)

Jimmy, eleven, just put his head down in his mashed potatoes and cried.

And our dramatic one, Debbie, eight, jumped from the table, knocked over her chair, ran to her room, and yelled, "I am never coming out!"

But as the days followed, our children began to get a little excited. They started to tell their friends that they were moving to Guatemala and had to learn Spanish.

That July we attended Brother Hagin's camp meeting in Tulsa. Jim volunteered to take care of the mission table for Rhema. One afternoon, a young man stopped by and asked Jim what he believed the Lord had called him to do. Jim told him with confidence that he was going to be a missionary in Guatemala.

"What type of vehicle are you taking?" the man asked.

Jim already knew the type of vehicle that he wanted to buy. He described a Jeep Cherokee and shared how much money we had saved to buy it. Jim had been saving money toward a vehicle from his construction work, and we were using my paychecks to pay bills and buy food. As the man listened, he began to smile. He had been a missionary in Guatemala and had the exact vehicle Jim was describing. It already had a Guatemalan license plate, and it was for sale.

We knew the Lord had set this up!

I packed up our house and set aside the items we wanted to take. I either sold or gave away many of our belongings. Jim traveled to some churches our Rhema classmates now pastored and shared about our move to Guatemala. He was able to raise about $250 in monthly cash support.

Then things began to happen quickly, as God was in all of this. We packed a five-by-eight-foot trailer with all our kitchen items, clothing, books, tapes, and Jim's motorcycle. We hitched the trailer to the Cherokee Jim had purchased from the missionary. We were ready to move forward.

12

OUR MISSIONARY ADVENTURE BEGINS

We left Tulsa early on a Thursday morning, October 9, 1979, and began our journey to Guatemala. As we arrived at the Texas/Mexico border, we had to unload everything while men looked through all our boxes. They detained us there for four hours. Despite this, I loved the trip through Mexico. I loved seeing the people, what they were doing, and how they lived. Most of the little pueblos were just like you see on television.

We didn't travel at night because of bandits and because we didn't know the roads. We had a Sanborn map and followed it all the way through Mexico. It told us which hotels were good and had drive-in courtyards where we could pull in our Jeep and trailer. It also indicated dips in the road, gas stations, and decent restaurants. Having this map with us was a tremendous blessing.

Ordering food was hilarious. We either pointed or said the words the best we could in Spanish. I remember at one restaurant, I asked for grape soda (*uva*) for the kids, and they brought out *cuba*, which was some type of alcohol. Of course, we had them take it back. I tried again, getting it right the second time.

Many Spanish words are similar to English. With others, changing only one letter changes the definition. For example, *pescado* is "fish" and *pecado* is "sin." *Hombre* is "man" and *hambre* is "hungry." *Arbejas* are "peas," *abeja* is "bee," and *ovejas* are "sheep." Another one that sometimes gave me a little problem: *harina* is "flour" and *arena* is "sand." One more: "to pray" is *orar* and "to cry" is *llorar*.

I remember one night when I wanted to greet the people. I thought the word *gritar* meant "greet," but it really means "to scream." So I was going to say to the people, "*Yo les grito en el nombre de Jesus,*" (I scream at you in the name of Jesus). Thankfully, a missionary woman corrected me before I got in front of the people.

Learning the Spanish language was not easy, but it is a must if a missionary wants to talk directly with the people. I have made hundreds of mistakes, but I've learned to laugh at myself and then get it right. I am still learning the language after all these years.

13

FIRST YEARS
ON THE MISSION FIELD

We spent our first years in Guatemala learning from our mistakes.

We rented a house on the outskirts of Quetzaltenango, which was not a good decision because we lived isolated from the people. Our children attended an English-speaking school that had been started for missionary children. They quickly adapted. Jim would leave with other missionaries to help with their work and to see what the Lord would speak to him. I was left alone in the house, and guess who came knocking at my door?

The Enemy—the devil. He said, "You have no friends in this place. You cannot even speak Spanish. You don't know how to barter for your food in the open market. You need to return to the United States."

I was in a battle between my flesh and my spirit. My flesh cried out, *Lord, get me out of this place!*

I don't want to be here. But my spirit said, *You are called to Guatemala.*

Satan tried to make me so miserable that we would pack up and move back to the US. I knew we were in the will of God. I knew we were supposed to be where we were. I admit it was hard for me. But if it was easy, anyone could do it.

I dried my eyes before picking up the children from school and before Jim got home. This happened day after day until one morning, while on my knees in prayer, I heard the Lord say in my spirit, *Stop this crying. Get up and do what I've called you to do.*

The next morning, I told Jim, "I'm going with you today. Whatever you are doing, I am going to do it with you."

He liked the idea of me getting out of the house so I could begin adjusting. He could see I was having a hard time.

I remember helping him pour a footer for someone's house, making visits, and talking with other missionaries. I invited some teachers from our children's school to our house for a Bible lesson. A few liked what they heard, but most of them did not. We were fresh out of Bible school and were zealous for good works. Most thought we were a cult because we believed in divine health, and we believed in the gifts of the Spirit. Jimmy's schoolteacher was extremely interested, and he wanted to hear more.

He kept coming to our house to ask questions and to learn. He even brought his wife with him. They ended up becoming missionaries with us.

We just began doing what we knew to do. We took our interpreter, Raul Sosa, with us and went from church to church—anywhere a door opened to us. Our family of five knew enough words to greet the people. We could sing one song in Spanish: "Yo Tengo un Amigo Que Me Ama—Su Nombre Es Jesus" ("I Have a Friend Who Loves Me and His Name Is Jesus"). We had reel-to-reel tapes of Reverend T. L. Osborn in Spanish. Jim preached the gospel using his interpreter. During our first year on the field, approximately three thousand people were led to the Lord. These were people in other pueblos outside of our city, and we put our trust in those pastors to follow up, keep them in their churches, and disciple them.

Two single women joined us as missionaries and then a family of four. For several weeks we held church in our home. Then a young man and two other women missionaries joined us. We moved our church services to the Bonifaz Hotel because we needed more space. There were no other English services in the area, and several other English-speaking missionaries of other denominations wanted to attend. The service was bilingual so our Guatemalan friends could come too.

More missionaries came on board. We left the Bonifaz Hotel after about one year and moved the church to a property belonging to Anita Gonzales, one of our English-speaking friends from England. We stayed there for about nine months before we outgrew the building and moved the church to a former skating rink on 23 Avenue. The skates were still there, so we decided to invite the youth from the school where our children attended.

On Saturday nights around twenty young people came to skate, have fun, laugh, and talk with their friends. After about an hour and a half, we had intermission. Jim shared a few minutes from the Word of God, and then we had more skating and more fun. Most of these young people were from missionary families of other denominations. We did this for about three months and then closed the skating part and sold the skates.

In our fourth year on the field, I began a weekly Bible study for women in this same building. I taught the women for several months, and then I began to put the Word into action. I visited a women's jail, a nursing home, and an orphanage, asking permission to bring a group of ladies to minister to them. They all accepted. So one week I would teach at our local facility, and then the following week we would visit one of the three places. We did this for about three years.

The nursing home had about twenty-five women. Some walked with canes, others sat and stared at us, and others were bedridden. Their living conditions were extremely poor. The smell was not pleasant. We sang some choruses, shared from the Word of God, and prayed for their needs. These precious women received the Lord repeatedly. They mostly wanted someone to come and sit by them and talk to them. At Christmastime, we took gifts and food, and it was such a delight to see their toothless smiles filled with much joy.

The orphanage housed around forty children, from babies to teens. A young girl from our church was gifted to minister to children, and she could make the kids laugh and learn as she taught them the Word. We often brought items sent from the US as a way to bless the children. One US church sent a pair of new shoes for each child. Christmas was big with the kids, and we celebrated with puppets, sometimes a clown, gifts for all, and a piñata filled with candy. My greatest delight was going to the nursery to hold the babies, love them, and play with them. After all these years, we still present a Christmas program there.

The women's jail was nothing like we have in the US. They shared a room with another inmate, and some even had a baby or a small child with them. This genuinely surprised me! Most of them probably had three or four older children at home as well, but the authorities allowed them to have only their baby or the youngest child with them. Some were there for only a month or two for stealing, and others for a longer period, depending on what they'd done.

They loved to sing and clap their hands with the music we played. Most were hungry to hear the Word, and we prayed with them. They let us have one-on-one conversations with them. One of their main prayer requests was for an early release. Most of the ladies received the Lord. At Christmastime, we took food, gifts, and baby gifts. The guards stamped our arms and asked to see our IDs as we went in.

After five years, in 1987 we moved from 23 Avenue to our new church building, which missionaries and church people helped to build. We have been there for thirty-four years and have seen our church grow from a few hundred people to now over fifteen hundred.

We took our children out of school when we held campaigns, which did not make their teachers happy. We felt that our children were called as missionaries, the same as we were. The school gave us a hard time, telling us, "If you take the children out on a test day, they'll get an F because they cannot make it up."

After a couple of years, we decided to begin our own Accelerated Christian Education (ACE) school on our Bible school campus, just for children. This was a good decision for the families and for their children's education. The principal and most of the teachers were US missionaries. Our missionaries taught the Bible class directly from the Bible, and one of our missionary men taught the physical education class. We had a basketball court and a big field for running and softball. We hired a Guatemalan for the Spanish class. Each child had their own cubicle. The ACE curriculum is done by paces, so the children could work at their own speed and even graduate early. Our three children and several others graduated from the ACE program.

This K–12 school continues today on our Bible school campus. Several local Guatemalan children who speak English attend our school, and several are from our local church. The missionary children we had in the beginning are all grown and have returned to the US.

Kimberly, Jimmy, and Debbie, along with other missionary children, ministered in the children's program in our local church under the direction of our missionary Carol Schlimmer. Carol's assistant was a young girl from our church who knew how to work effectively with children, and she was dynamic.

She later became the children's pastor. At that time, only missionary children participated in this ministry. They performed dramas and skits, worked with puppets, dressed as clowns, interpreted for others, and did whatever Miss Carol needed them to do.

We began to hold monthly evangelistic meetings throughout Guatemala in a tent donated from a church stateside. In the afternoon, we held special children's services, and the missionary kids would minister. The children packed the tent and listened with enthusiasm as the puppets talked and said funny things. The children laughed and had a good time, singing action songs and watching the clowns dance with the music. They always gave the children the opportunity to ask Jesus into their heart after the mini message. They lifted their little hands and repeated a prayer.

Before the night service, the missionaries passed out tracts and invited people to come under the big tent to hear the Word of God and to be healed. More people attended services held in a tent or a building rather than in a local church. Jim, or another missionary, preached and then gave an altar call and prayed for the sick. We saw many healed.

We began to have groups come from the US to be a part of our evangelistic meetings. On this one occasion, Jim's brother, Jerry, was part of the US group. He prayed for a mute boy. When this little boy was four years old, he witnessed his father's murder by a machete, and a spirit of fear came upon the boy. The father died, and the boy never spoke again. When he came to the night service, he was now a few years older. He heard the Word of God preached and the words spoken by the missionary: "God loves you and wants to meet your need."

He went forward for prayer and believed that he would speak again. The little boy did not say anything after Jerry prayed for him and returned to his seat. Suddenly, a commotion started in the corner.

This young boy had begun to speak.

His mother asked him questions, and he answered. All the people around him knew he had not been able to speak. Jesus had healed him, and the people began praising the Lord. It was glorious!

14

OUR VISION UNFOLDS

One night the Lord woke Jim up and told him, *Take a pen and paper and write the vision of Living Water Teaching.* It was a six-point vision that has guided this ministry for the last forty-two years, even after Jim's passing:

1. Convert my people to the Word, not to religion.

2. Train them in righteousness.

3. By example show them my power to change their lives by giving spiritual conditioning to their spirits by way of the Word.

4. Train my sent ones to go on and do greater things than I have shown you by building on your errors and successes.

5. The vision is transferable, but my commission is not! You are to carry it forth into all of Latin America.

6. Trouble the waters of Latin America as the angel troubled the waters of Bethesda. Trouble them with faith, healing, and salvation.

We began our own Bible school in 1981 in a rented house around the corner from our home. We had twenty-six Guatemalan students. Many more attended in the second year, and then the numbers kept multiplying. We moved to bigger facilities closer to downtown Xela. We held classes upstairs in a rented house, and some missionaries lived downstairs.

Most all the missionaries taught either one or two classes. Jim and I both had classes, and it was such a delight to see understanding dawn in the eyes and faces of the students. We taught classes on prayer, the Holy Spirit, healing, the name of Jesus, spiritual gifts, our identity in Christ, marriage and the family, and so much more.

Other missionaries came on board who had a call to other countries in Latin America. Eventually, we had directors trained under Living Water Teaching opening branches in Costa Rica, Honduras, Panama, El Salvador, Nicaragua, and Mexico. The Lord spoke to others about joining Living Water Teaching and taking the vision to other nations, like Paraguay, Columbia, Africa, Japan, Belize, Peru, and Germany.

In the last few years, the ministry has expanded to Haiti, Bolivia, and the Dominican Republic. Since the inception of Living Water Teaching, we have had over 44,000 Bible school graduates who now teach and preach the good news of the gospel to the glory of God.

We have had directors come to Guatemala and fulfill the vision the Lord gave them. Some returned to the US afterward, while others continued with their mission work independent of Living Water Teaching. Today, Living Water continues with the vision of training students in the Word of God and stirring the waters of Latin America with faith, healing, and salvation in the countries of Belize, Bolivia, the Dominican Republic, El Salvador, Guatemala, Haiti, Honduras, Mexico, Nicaragua, Panama, and Paraguay.

In 1983, we began to look at land to build a Bible school with dorms for students, a kitchen and dining room, laundry facilities, a construction/maintenance area, a mechanic shop, an ACE Academy for our children's education, and missionary housing. We found a piece of property with twenty-two acres, prayed over it, and had complete peace in our hearts to begin to build as funds became available.

We began with one building paid for by our partners. We used the building as offices and then shortly began on the second building. We moved the offices to the second building and put the ACE Academy in the first. To make a long story short, we turned the first two buildings into a girls' dorm and boys' dorm and continued building as money became available.

We now have thirty-six buildings on our Bible school campus. Several years back, we constructed two new dorms for our Bible school students, paid for by Gary and Pat VanderPol. The girls' dorm is called Star 1 in honor of their son, Tom VanderPol, who died in the airplane crash. *Star* comes from the initials representing each family member: S for Shayla (daughter), T for Tom, A for Ahna (daughter), and R for Renae (Tom's wife). The second dorm is named Star 2.

Gary and Pat also gave funds to expand our much-needed Bible school facility because of its increasing growth. On the second floor, we added two new classrooms, a library, men's and women's bathrooms, and a sitting area with couches and chairs. On the first floor, we have a room for activities, meetings, and banquets. We have restrooms for men and women near a large foyer, where we have held weddings and other large gatherings. We are truly thankful for the generous love gifts Gary and Pat VanderPol have given to Living Water Teaching.

Jim wrote several books, one of which was titled *With Signs Following*. I want to relate one of the miracles we experienced. As Jim wrote in the above-mentioned book, "Miracles are most often immediate and instantaneous! They are breathtaking, heart-stopping interventions of God that stop all questions and render all doubt as ineffective."

When we began developing our Bible school campus in Quetzaltenango, Guatemala, in 1983 we knew that pure drinking water would be one of our biggest challenges. The Quetzaltenango Valley lies eight thousand feet in the Sierra Madre Mountains, and the water table is low most of the year. During the best of times, we could expect three to five months of water rationing, perhaps with a flow of half a gallon per minute and then only six to eight hours per day. The municipality required us to run lines from the main system to our campus, but seldom did anything come through. We carried water in fifteen-gallon plastic containers by the truckful, day after day.

I inquired about digging a well but was told there was no water anywhere in the area. No one had been successful in digging a well, nor in finding water. Geologists and hydrologists said it would be useless. The man who owned a drilling rig in Quetzaltenango said he would charge $17,000 to drill a test hole whether he found water or not.

He told several people, "What choice do they have but me? I am going to stick them good."

He did not like evangelical Christians or North Americans, and his extreme price was his way of sarcastically expressing it.

I prayed, *Lord, I just feel in my heart that you want us to have our own water supply independent of man's system and the weather. Show me where we should dig a well. Men have said and even proven that there is no water here in the area, but I believe it's your will for Living Water Teaching Bible School to have its own source of water.*

The answer as to where to dig the well did not come immediately. I walked the land. I talked and prayed with the missionaries and staff in the construction department. When no answer came, I did what I knew to do next—looked for men to dig the hole.

The construction people came to me asking, "Where do we start?"

I remember asking them to give me a few minutes while I collected my thoughts. I closed my office door and prayed, *Lord, where is the water?*

His answer was clear. *Where do you want the well? Where will it be the most convenient? Since there is no water here, I'll put the water where you put the well.*

I went immediately out to the waiting workers and walked to the site—the piece of ground that the Lord had shown me where He would put the water—which is now by the basketball court and in the area where we built our prayer chapel. The hired crew and some of our own construction team began to dig with a chisel and hammer. We used no modern equipment; we dug it all by hand.

The hole was one meter across, which is about thirty-nine inches. The first part of the digging (less than twenty feet) went rapidly, then we hit solid rock! Granite! The workers automatically assumed I wanted to quit. It would be too expensive and time consuming to go on. Since the rock was granite, no water could penetrate it; neither would water be found beyond it.

I simply remembered the Lord's words, *Where do you want it?*

We had them continue digging, and dig they did—by hand with chisel and hammer, month after month. We went through crew after crew, pumping air to them when they hit gas pockets. We ran electrical lights. We lowered them to their work and pulled them out using a rope tied to a winch.

People laughed and made fun of the idea, including some of our own staff. Comments were made about hitting China and digging for gold. They attributed the foolishness to us and called it Zirkle's folly. However, because they were well paid by a gringo, they continued to dig. Even some of our missionaries got in on the fun. However, Jim knew he had heard correctly from the Lord, and seventeen months later, we hit water. Sweet, wet water. Through solid granite rock ran a stream of water at a depth of 385 feet. This well is one of the deepest man-made, hand-dug wells in history, and we have it on our campus in Quetzaltenango, Guatemala.

The well is operated by a pump lowered by a cable. It pumps the water into a container, and another pump passes water through the pipes that run into our buildings. All of our buildings have water, but there have been times during the dry season (November through April) when hardly any rain falls, and the well runs dry. There are other times when we have large groups staying on campus, and very little water comes in. We then have to have water hauled in, in big trucks. Several times our construction team has dug a little deeper to receive more water.

The shaft is clean, straight, and dressed from the top down, which means they took a shovel, smoothed out the sides, and packed the dirt solid so no loose dirt would fall as they went down and came back up. It's right where God said it would be—exactly where we wanted it. No one doubts that it was a miracle. We have water most of the year, sweet and clear. We've since dug a second well, also where we needed it. This well is 430 feet deep and took eighteen months to dig through solid rock. The second well was just as much a miracle as the first.

The well on our Bible school campus

Pastor Jim shared many more miracles in his book *With Signs Following*. Another miracle we saw involved my mom, Jane. My mom was in her mid-fifties, and she had visited the mission field several times before she decided to become a missionary with us. She had to go through the same kind of training as all the other missionaries, and she raised her own support. She came for three years and wore many different hats, as all the missionaries do: she worked in our two annual medical clinics, helped serve food at the monthly men's breakfasts for the homeless, helped pass out tracts before evangelistic services, and managed the kitchen.

One day she went to the market to buy food and encountered a great commotion as she exited. "My baby is dead!" a woman screamed.

Mom pushed her way through the crowd and took the baby in her arms. She began speaking life over the child, binding death in the name of Jesus Christ. As she continued to pray, the precious little child began to breathe and then cried for its mother. To the glory of God, life had returned to the baby. A notable miracle—yes, indeed!

In the chaos of the situation, Mom had thrown down her purchased items and her purse, but surprisingly, no one had stolen her belongings. Really two miracles happened that day: most importantly, the baby returned to life, but also Mom got her purse and her purchased items back.

My mom, Jane

This was the first time the Lord used my mom in this supernatural way. However, on another occasion, the Lord used Mom to stir up faith in our son. Jimmy was in his teen years when he actually saw his own faith work for him. He had a boxer dog named Buck that he had brought from the US. Jimmy was very proud of him and loved him very much. Buck was an active dog and unusually attractive in his brutish beauty. More than once, people had tried to steal him, so Jimmy checked on him first thing nearly every morning.

Jim and I had gone to the States while my mom took care of the children in our absence. One morning Jimmy came crying into the house, pulling his dog with him. Someone had evidently poked out his beloved Buck's eye with a stick. The eye socket was completely empty. Mom comforted him as best she could and then suggested they pray together. They laid hands on Buck, praying that God would restore the eye.

They put Buck back out in the yard and didn't check on him again until feeding time later that afternoon. Jimmy went to the yard with the dog food but soon ran back into the house, yelling, "Grandma, Grandma, Buck has his eye! God gave him back his eye!"

Mom inspected the eye, and it was fixed back into position just like the other one, and it was completely normal.

15

MEETING OPPOSITION

Our first years in Guatemala were very troubled with a lot of terrorist-type fighting happening. The Guatemalan Civil War was fought from 1960–1996 between the government of Guatemala and various leftist rebel groups, which were primarily supported by ethnic Maya indigenous peoples and Ladino peasants. The struggle was based on long-standing issues of unfair land distribution.

The Civil War started on November 13, 1960, when a group of left-wing junior military officers led a failed revolt against the government of General Fuentes. In the 1970s, social discontent continued among the large populations of indigenous people and peasants. Many organized into insurgent groups and began to resist the government forces. During the 1980s, the Guatemalan military assumed almost absolute governmental power for five years. It had successfully infiltrated and eliminated enemies in every socio-political institution of the nation, including the political, social, and intellectual classes. In the final stage of the war, the military developed a parallel, semi-visible, low profile but high-effect control of Guatemala's national life. It is estimated that 140,000 to 200,000 people were killed or forcefully "disappeared" during the conflict (per bing.com and en.wikipedia.org).

In the early 1980s, we were invited to evangelize in a city called Tejutla. We took another missionary family with us, and as we pulled into town, we came up against a long metal pole across our path. Several young men in their early twenties paced around, carrying machine guns.

They ordered us to drive to the town square and told us that all the village had been called together for instruction and recruiting. We were met by Communist insurgents who escorted our men and children to the fountain area of the square while the missionary's wife and I stayed in the Jeep to guard our belongings. I noticed a few young girls in uniform also carrying guns.

A Cuban soldier stood on the town square's fountain, making a propaganda speech to the people who had been forced by gunpoint to listen to his message. He began to slander the United States and the North Americans who had come to Guatemala to tell them about God.

An older woman came over and sat at Jim's feet. Soon a local pastor we had worked with and around forty others followed. The people did not like what the Communist guerillas said about us because they knew us. We had held a medical campaign in this town a year earlier, giving free medical treatment and free medication and loving and praying for the people. Very quietly, our team slipped out, got in the car, and went to the pastor's home. We kept looking back, checking that the insurgents hadn't followed us. We spent the night with the pastor's family and prayed for safety for the whole town. The following day the children presented a drama, Jim preached the Word, there were many healings, and people were greatly ministered to.

We began holding clinics in various parts of Guatemala, never charging the people for anything—checkups, medications, tooth extractions. Our group members from the US brought some of the medications we used, and we bought the rest.

After our clinics were over and we'd left the area, we often heard that the Communist guerillas took the medicine away from the people. We were not able to hold our medical campaigns during times of uprisings and shootings. When the city was put on curfew, we had to be off the streets by dark.

In 1982, a group came from the US to participate in one of our evangelistic campaigns. Jim's brother, Jerry, and sister-in-law, Linda, stayed with us. I had left the office and planned to go by the store to pick up an item at lunchtime. As I traveled down the main street in front of the open market, people pulled down their storefronts (large metal doors like we would have on a garage) and yelled, "Get off the street!"

I asked, "What's going on?"

Again, they said, "Get off the street!"

I drove as fast as I could to our children's school where I ran into a friend from church, Anita Gonzalez, who told me a coup was taking place. At the time, I had no idea what that was. She told me to get my kids and get home and off the streets as quickly as possible. I hurried my three children into the car, along with some other missionary children, and headed for the house. We heard gunfire for what seemed like hours. We all sat on the floor in a bedroom where we felt safest from any stray bullets.

Jerry got his guitar and began to sing to calm the children and my racing heart. Hours later the children's parents came to pick them up, and Jim came home. He had learned that the young military was trying to oust the old established military. He wasn't sure how many were killed.

It was a thirty-six-year war. Thousands of people were killed during those years. Over two hundred thousand children were left fatherless or homeless. Many of those children lived on the streets and ate the food the markets threw out or stole food. They slept in doorways, on park benches, or in boxes on the sidewalk. Many war widows sent their children to the streets to beg and steal. Some mothers even sold their daughters into prostitution. They did whatever it took to eat and stay alive. We were blessed to take food and clothing to the two orphanages that took in many of these children. We also gave food to children who lived on the streets. Hundreds of these homeless children lived in Guatemala City.

Through the Marion Zirkle Children's Foundation, our humanitarian side of the ministry, we have blessed countless children with food, clothing, and shoes. We've given at least eight wheelchairs to children, paid for a brain scan for a child, and given hundreds of eyeglasses and countless vitamins. In Nicaragua, we helped supplement education for three hundred fifty children, built a new classroom, and bought ten ceiling fans.

Every Christmas we bless approximately ten thousand babies, children, and youth with toys or a shoebox full of useful items and toys. Our partners in the United States have helped us fill shoeboxes for the last twenty-four years.

Other partners and businesses send bulk items. We receive boxes of coloring books and crayons, hair items for girls and teens, water pistols, toy guns, dolls, pens, pencils, notebooks, stuffed animals, cars, clothing, diapers, bottles, rattles, and other varieties of toys. We receive thousands of candy canes and other types of candy and try to make sure all the children get some. The US staff makes a manifest of all that comes in, and then they pack the shoeboxes and bulk items on pallets to be sent on containers to Guatemala. Once our US staff locates a shipping company and sets the date to load, our people are given only two hours to load everything. They all give a sigh of relief when the containers are on their way.

We have been sending two forty-foot containers for the last twenty-plus years. They come by ship and arrive at one of the Guatemala ports. Then they're brought by trucks to our Bible school campus in Xela, and most of our staff is needed to help sort the donations and organize the shoeboxes according to age and gender.

The donors mark each shoebox, indicating *niña* (girl) or *niño* (boy) and age group (0–16). We also fill shoeboxes ourselves with the donated bulk items and candy, according to age and gender.

We usually appoint two people to scout communities and schools for areas with a low standard of living that would especially benefit from the shoebox donations. Our staff, along with a visiting group from the US of about twenty-five to sixty people, delivers the shoeboxes and presents a program, including a drama, Christmas carols in Spanish, puppets, a mini message, and an altar call. The children are so excited, they can hardly sit still, knowing they're going to receive gifts. If we're at a school of older children, we present a different kind of program. After the program, we divide the teens into groups, and then the missionaries and group members talk to each group individually. At times, it is one-on-one ministry.

We always receive requests for several thousand more toys from churches, organizations, and others that minister to children. We help as much as we can and as far as the toys will reach. The Lord always supplies! I am always blessed by the children's excitement and by the opportunity to minister to so many people. Every year, an average of 2,500 people receive the Lord during this outreach.

Operation Christmas Shoebox

117

Guatemala is primitive in comparison to standards in the United States. Some of the people we minister to still live in homes with dirt floors and no running water. Many places have no electricity or have their electricity rationed and have power only for a few hours each day. The women in the small villages wash their clothes with water from a lake or a river. Some areas have a center set up with several washboards called *pilas*, where the women get together to talk and laugh while they work. They spread the washed clothing on the grass or over fences to dry.

Most of the women have four to seven children, and many also have a baby tied to their backs while they do their chores. In other families, the oldest girl in the family—maybe only seven or eight years old—helps her mother by tying her baby sister or brother on her own back. They use a typical cloth, which is a colorful piece of fabric about six feet long and six feet wide. They tie the cloth in such a way that the baby can't fall out. It's also long enough to cover the baby when it falls asleep.

The women work ridiculously hard for many long hours every day and are often out in the sun all day working in the fields. Some forty-year-old women look fifty-five or sixty. The men are also very industrious, working in the fields from sunup to sundown.

16

LEARNING TO ADJUST

One of my biggest challenges when we first moved to Guatemala was learning how to barter in the open market.

I remember the awful smell as I entered with my basket. It could have been the odor of dried blood from the hanging meat, rotten potatoes, unwashed bodies, or a mixture of many stenches under the same roof. I wanted to hold my nose, but instead I held my breath. I did not want to be the *ugly American*, as some from the US have been called.

Stray dogs ran wild through the market. Mothers openly nursed their babies. I saw dozens of food choices, including every kind of vegetable and fruit imaginable. Vendor after vendor enticed people to buy from them. Usually, when a *gringa* (girl or woman from the US or Europe) wants to make a purchase, the seller begins at a higher price, and the gringa bargains and offers less. The two barter back and forth until a price is agreed upon.

I learned how to barter and soon left the market with my basket full of the best vegetables and fruit imaginable, with very little spent. In 1979, corn for tortillas was three cents a pound, and black beans cost five cents a pound. Now, corn is Q2.00, which equals about twenty-eight cents, and black beans are eighty cents.

Meat hangs in slabs on large hooks. The meat was the worst part of the market for me. I saw pig heads and pig tails and all kinds of gruesome-looking stuff. I found a good meat man and learned how to say, "*Dos libras de carne de molida, por favor,*" translated "Two pounds of ground beef, please." After all these years, I still buy from the same meat place, but his children now run the shop. They have always been fair with me. They cut a nice portion off the slab and run it through the grinder twice. We used to get good hamburger meat at seventy-five cents per pound. Now it is around Q28.00, which equals around $3.68, depending on the exchange rate. During our first few years in the field, the dollar and the quetzal were of equal value. At this moment, we receive Q7.60 to $1.00.

I also shop at the outside market where streets are lined with vendors selling beautiful tomatoes, broccoli, cauliflower, lettuce, watermelon, canta-loupe, pineapple, strawberries, bananas, plantains, onions, potatoes—the list could go on and on. Produce in the market area is plentiful, but the grocery store is another story, as these stores are quite small and don't sell everything we're used to buying.

I remember that I once wanted salad dressing. I tried to explain to the store owner what I wanted by using all kinds of hand motions and saying *ensalada*, which is Spanish for salad. He showed me one item after another to no avail. I think he was frustrated; I know I was.

About that time, I heard someone speaking English, and I gave silent thanks to Jesus. I asked her to help me tell the owner what I wanted. She did, but he answered, "No, we don't have anything like that." I found out pretty quick that I was going to have to change some of my recipes.

Shopping for food took most of the morning. If I wanted chicken, I had to go where they sold chicken. If I wanted bread, I went to the bread store. They didn't sell a lot of sandwich bread, and what they had was very hard with a little soft area in the middle. Making sandwiches for the children's lunches was a big hassle because they could enjoy only about a third of the sandwich.

Arriving home from the market, I had to clean all the fruit and vegetables with Clorox or a special liquid called Liquid Organic Cleaner (LOC). Because of what they use to grow the fruit and vegetables, you can contract amoebas, which are single-celled microscopic animals that can cause nausea, vomiting, bloating, and a rotten-egg taste in the mouth, if the produce isn't washed properly.

One of my greatest blessings was hiring someone to help me with the shopping, cleaning the vegetables, housework, washing, ironing, etc. A missionary of another denomination was leaving the field and asked if I wanted someone to help me in the house. I gave her a big, emphatic, "Yes!"

Berta was well trained in the kitchen. She could make great tortillas, picante sauce, plantains with black beans, and *paches*/tamales (cooked potatoes mashed or rice mixed with a good sauce, spices, a piece of chicken in the middle and steamed in banana leaves), along with other typical food. She was a good housekeeper and great all-around helper.

Eventually, bigger supermarkets replaced the smaller ones. Berta and I went shopping together every Monday morning. I dropped her off at the market with two big baskets while I went to the supermarket. Women always waited in the market area to carry customers' baskets to earn some money to feed their families. I was blessed to have two women who waited for us every Monday for many years to carry the baskets for Berta, because

I always gave them more money than some of the Guatemalan women did. I then returned to the market area to pick her up, pay the two women, and head for home. Berta cleaned all the fruit and vegetables while I put up the other items.

Berta has been with me for thirty-six years. She is a good Christian woman and attends the Assembly of God church. She has been like family, not a *muchacha* (maid). She has helped me with Spanish, and we have prayed together many times and discussed a few things from the Word of God. She is my shopping partner and so much more. She recently turned eighty-four but still wants to work in my kitchen. I've had to hire a younger woman, Yolanda, to help with the housekeeping, along with her husband, Rene, who has been our gardener for many years. Berta's daughter is the children's pastor in our local church.

Working full-time in the ministry, it has been an extreme blessing to have help in my home, and many of our missionaries feel the same. The rate of monthly pay for someone working in the home is around two hundred dollars. These workers are a blessing to the people they work for, but they, in turn, are blessed as well with a job. Rene arrives at seven in the morning, and Berta and Yolanda arrive around eight. I always have bread and hot coffee waiting for them. They also eat lunch at my house and work until around two. When we arrive home around five, the house is clean, and Berta has supper in the oven. We have the evening to relax. Economically, it is worth it.

We have seen Quetzaltenango change right before our eyes. The Word of God brought prosperity to this nation through the thousands of students we have trained in the Word of God, through the other Bible schools in our city, and now by way of cable television, computers, internet, and radio programs from preachers all over the world. Most of the pastors here preach the Word of God instead of religion. In 1979, Guatemala was 3 percent Christian. Now, it is over 50 percent. Guatemala City has a couple of megachurches with over twenty-five thousand in attendance.

The peace treaty was signed in December 1996. Before that time no one wanted to invest in Guatemala because Communism tried to infiltrate the nation. But we strongly believe that didn't happen because of the Word of God and the strong Christians who live in the nation. There are a small percentage of Guatemalans who are financially blessed. Some have coffee *fincas* (farms), and others have large sugar cane plantations and export sugar all over the world. They travel back and forth to the US and Europe and have seen what their investments in their own nation can bring about. They have built beautiful malls, supermarkets, and stores like Walmart, Payless Shoes, and Sears, along with fast-food chains like Wendy's, McDonald's, Burger King, Pizza Hut, Domino's, Little Caesars, and Taco Bell, to name a few.

When we first moved to Guatemala in 1979, there were no fast-food chains in our city. They had places that sold pizza, Guatemala style, that sufficed for the moment, but we wanted some good ole' North American food. The kids got so excited when we were in Guatemala City and stopped at McDonald's for lunch. We could hardly wait for one to come to our city, and it finally did. Now that there are so many good places to eat in Xela, we never go to McDonald's.

One thing I missed the most from the US was chocolate. How I craved a Snickers bar. We stopped at a gas station one day, and Jim bought a little box of Baby Ruth candy bars. We looked forward to that taste of chocolate. When I ripped off the wrapper, I saw bugs inside. We were all so disappointed.

Many Guatemalans also travel to the United States and places in Europe to study and get their degrees. I know of successful doctors, dentists, engineers, restaurant owners, and others who moved to the US for a few years, got their degree, and then returned to Guatemala to begin their practice or start up their business.

Guatemala has a population of 17 million, and 59.3 percent of the population live below the poverty line. In addition, 23 percent live in extreme poverty. The primary causes of poverty in Guatemala are its economic, social, and land inequality rates, which are among the highest in the world. It is estimated that the top 5 percent control or own more than 85 percent of the wealth in Guatemala.

17

ANOINTED STAFF MINISTERS

The local church that Living Water Teaching founded continues to grow. Pastor Wilson and Maytte Moir have been the pastors for the last twenty years. Pastor Wilson graduated from our Bible school. Attendance at the church has grown from a few hundred people to over fifteen hundred in the three Sunday services. The Wednesday night service is basically full as well.

We also have an anointed praise and worship leader, Jairo Talé, and he has a dynamic team to work with and knows how to lead us into the presence of God. Our children's pastor, Thelma Diaz, has been with us for fifteen years and has a unique style of ministering to children using humor as she teaches Bible stories.

Our youth are becoming well-disciplined under the leadership of our pastor's son, Wilson Rafael. They are growing in their walk with God and increasing in their faith through Bible-centered teachings. Today, we have one hundred fifty youth who meet weekly to worship God.

Another part of my vision for the ministry was to open an orphanage on our Bible school campus. The vision was fulfilled in January 2017 when we opened our orphanage (or temporary home) called The Promised Home. We have had several hundred abused or abandoned babies and children in the home at different times during the last five years. One precious little boy was put in a big black garbage bag and left beside the garbage bins. A man was cleaning up around that area and heard the faint cry of a baby coming from the bag. After finding the newborn boy inside the bag, he contacted authorities, who took the baby to the hospital. Soon a judge contacted our temporary home to see if we would take the baby until family could be located. He was soon adopted by a nice family. Another darling newborn baby boy was found alongside a road in a rural area, and a woman on her way to work found him. He also was sent to our orphanage, and he is still with us. He is contented and has cute, rosy cheeks. His smile will melt your heart.

One baby girl was found on the floor of an ATM room. Another baby was left in a ditch. We received twins who were left in a hospital after birth. Two little boys arrived in our care after the police took them off the street for selling items so their family could eat. We have also received babies who were removed from alcoholic parents, as well as from families who could not provide for their children.

The Lord has given us the privilege of loving and caring for these precious little ones. Several children have been adopted. The majority of the children that we have received may have only spent a few nights in The Promised Home before the judge transferred them to another facility or they were awarded to a family member. Those still with us continue to receive tender, loving care.

Pastor Ubaldo and his wife, Guisela, are the directors of the orphanage. They are also missionaries with Living Water Teaching. They have several nurses on staff and another four or five employees who work around the clock to care for the children. I have had the privilege of visiting as much as I desire. The children there call me *Abuelita* (little grandmother). I usually go twice a week and take some fruit and other goodies. I play with the older ones and help feed and hold the smaller children and babies. Loving these precious little ones helps me not to miss my great-grandchildren so much.

Before we opened the orphanage, we had the opportunity to take in two sets of children who had been abandoned by their mother. The first was a family of six: three boys and three girls, ranging from three years of age to teenagers. The Marion Zirkle Children's Foundation took on the responsibility of caring for these children through helping provide for their schooling, clothing, food, utilities, and a full-time live-in maid under the supervision of one of our missionary couples.

One of our missionary ladies met another family of five kids in our local church. They had also been abandoned by their mother, who went to the United States and left them in the care of their grandfather. The oldest girl was twenty-three years old and assumed the motherhood role taking care of them. They lived in very poor conditions. This missionary asked me if we would consider letting them move into the house with the other children. At this time, three of the older children of the first family had already moved out and begun their own lives.

This second family ranged in age from thirteen to twenty-three years of age. We helped the youngest two finish their studies. The foundation also provided full care until, one by one, they found jobs and left. Three are married and now have babies of their own. The oldest girl is not married and works in our finance department. The three-year-old of the first family is now in his thirties and works in our multimedia department. They both call me Mom.

18

WHAT IS REAL MISSIONS?

Is missions about feeding the hungry, building orphanages, building churches, and having relief programs and benevolence funds? Is it about running clothing drives to cover the naked? Organizing bread or soup lines? Creating groups of doctors, dentists, nurses, caring and loving people?

No. Missions is about preaching the gospel. Romans 1:16 (KJV) says, "For it [the gospel] is the power of God unto salvation." The gospel is good news. The gospel in one word is *Jesus*. In three words: *God loves you*. In five words: *Jesus died for your sins*. The gospel is summed up in one powerful Scripture: John 3:16. It tells us the purpose of missions: "For God so loved the world that He gave His only begotten Son, that whoever believes in Him should not perish but have everlasting life."

Who can fathom the depth of God's love, which made Him willing to give His only Son to come to this earth to die on the cross, to have His body bruised, beaten, and battered for our healing and divine health? This love forced the Father to see His Son's precious blood shed as the crown of thorns was pressed into his skull, spikes were driven through his hands and feet, thirty-nine stripes ripped open His back, and a spear pierced His precious side. He did this for the whole world.

Jesus came so all the world, whoever would believe in Him, would have eternal life. When we think of the world, we think of the drunkard, the prostitute, the drug dealer, the killer, and the liar. But the world is anyone who is lost—anyone who has never received Jesus as their Savior.

After the resurrection of Jesus and before His ascension back to the Father, He gave us the Great Commission not once but five times. He repeated it in each of the four Gospels and in the first chapter of the book of Acts. He gave it on different occasions and in various places:

- Matthew 28:16—Jesus commissioned His disciples from a mountain in Galilee.
- Mark 16:14—He appeared to the eleven while they were eating.

- Luke 24:33–36—Jesus appeared to the eleven as they were gathered together in Jerusalem.

- John 20:19—He came and stood in the midst of the disciples, appearing despite the closed, locked doors.

- Acts 1:8—Jesus told them of the gift of the Holy Spirit and gave the Great Commission from the Mount of Olives.

The Great Commission contains two primary parts: the preaching of the gospel around the world and the making of disciples. If Jesus lives in your heart, you are a missionary. If He does not live in your heart, you are a mission field. The mission of the church is missions. The idea of missions was born in the heart of God. God's mission and passion are found in 2 Peter 3:9: "The Lord is not slack concerning His promise, as some count slackness, but is longsuffering toward us, not willing that any should perish but that all should come to repentance."

Many Christians are called, equipped, and gifted, but they sit on a church pew with their arms folded, waiting for God to tell them what to do. But He already did that when He said, "Go into all the world and preach, teach, baptize, heal the sick, and make disciples" (Mark 16:15–18, author's paraphrase).

19

OUR GOD RESTORES

At the writing of this book, it has been almost twenty-three years since the accident. By the grace of God, the vision of Living Water Teaching continues. We have experienced His abundant life, His abundant grace, and His abundant goodness. To date, we have seen more than eight hundred thousand children, teens, and adults brought into the kingdom of God.

My husband Jim gave 100 percent of his time, love, and energy in the nineteen years that he served as a missionary in Guatemala. He did more in his nineteen years of ministry than most men do in their entire lives. He, as the founder of Living Water Teaching, was also a pastor, evangelist, apostle, pilot, man of God, strong leader, author, husband, father, grandfather, and so much more. Jim was a visionary, and he shared about missions and preached in almost every state as well as in several countries outside the US.

Dr. Lester Sumrall stated, "In my fifty-nine years of ministry, I have never seen missions done better." Rev. Kenneth Copeland shared, "Jim Zirkle is an apostle and prophet of God for Central America. We are proud to invest and support the work of Living Water Teaching." Pastor Billy Joe Daugherty of Tulsa, Oklahoma, stated, "Jim Zirkle and Living Water Teaching are training ministers to be effective on the field. They are not only reaching thousands by evangelism, but their schools have made true discipleship a reality." Oral Roberts University conferred an honorary Doctor of Divinity degree upon Jim for developing effective methods of training missionaries.

Jim laid the foundation for what we have continued to build upon. Our Father God has shown Himself forever faithful.

Kimberly, my oldest daughter, was married to Chris Hamberger, the photographer on the medical campaign who died in the crash. Later she married Dany Mejia, a missionary who served for many years with Living Water Teaching and who was also on that medical trip in Playa Grande. He was in the caravan, driving with the other missionaries and staff. They have been married for nineteen years and have a beautiful daughter named Daniela. Dany helped raise Chris's children, now grown: Christopher, Matthew, and Lynsey. They have four grandchildren. Dany and Kimberly currently work as administrators in our ministry in Guatemala. They wear many different hats. Dany is a graduate of our Bible school and has been a missionary with Living Water Teaching for twenty-one years.

My daughter-in-law, Laura, who was married to our son, Jimmy, pilot on the DC-3 aircraft, is now married to a Guatemalan man named Manuel Sarti. They worked several years as missionaries with Living Water Teaching before moving to the United States. Manuel was a great interpreter and worked in various areas of the ministry. Laura was the principal of our ACE Academy. They have been married for twenty years. Together they have a beautiful daughter named Adrienne. Manuel has been a great father to Jimmy's three children, now all grown: Jimmy III, Alexis, and Jordan. They have four grandchildren.

I will always be grateful to these two men for stepping in, providing for, and loving Jimmy's and Chris's children—my adorable grandchildren.

Renae VanderPol, who was married to Tom, pilot on the DC-3 and missionary for several years, is now married to Aaron Timmermans. They have two boys of their own and raised Tom's two girls, Shayla and Ahna. Renae returned to the US after the accident and lives happily with her family. They have one granddaughter to date.

Miriam, a missionary with Living Water Teaching who oversaw our medical department at the time of the crash and who was married to pilot and missionary Raul Jacobs who died in the crash, has always been a treasured friend of mine. Their three children have all married, and she has several grandchildren. Miriam visits often with her three children; the youngest daughter lives in the US.

I did not think I would remarry. I closed my heart for a time. It took all I had to step into Jim's shoes and continue the ministry. However, about four years after the accident, I began to pray, *Lord, if it is Your will that I remarry, please let me marry the right man.* I knew I had to be careful. I did not want someone to come in and try to change the vision of Living Water Teaching. I prayed a lot, and God answered my prayers.

The Lord sent a very handsome man, Clarence, from the US on three medical/evangelistic trips to Guatemala before I gave him any notice. On his third trip, our spirits connected. Emails flew back and forth every day as we got to know each other. He had to learn how to use a computer. On one of my trips back to the US office in Caddo Mills, he came from Tulsa so we could get to know each other better. He told me he believed the Lord wanted him to be a part of Living Water Teaching. We had some good times together, and at the same time, we both prayed that we would hear clearly from the Lord.

Clarence is from a very close-knit family of four brothers and five sisters. His father was a pastor as well as two of his brothers. Clarence has one daughter married, three grandsons and three great-grandchildren, and one son.

My two girls wanted me to marry again, and they said my face radiated with the joy and happiness Clarence brought into my life. They also knew I needed help in taking the ministry to another level. His gifts and anointings have added so much to the ministry.

After much prayer, we truly believed God sent Clarence to Guatemala to be my husband and to join the ministry of Living Water Teaching. He returned to Guatemala a few months later and asked me out to dinner. As we were talking, he pulled out a Walmart bag with a necklace-sized box inside. My first thought was that he had bought me a necklace. However, inside was a smaller box with a ring. He proposed, and I said yes.

In Guatemala, you must have a civil wedding performed by a lawyer. This is the marriage recognized by the government. It is up to the couple to have the wedding in a church. Of course, Clarence and I both wanted to be married in our local church with our congregation. Now the fun began as we made wedding plans.

I wanted my two girls and their husbands, my daughter-in-law and her husband, my twelve grandchildren, my sister Linda, and Clarence's daughter and husband and grandson to be part of the wedding party. I chose fuchsia for the color of the girl's dresses, from the oldest all the way down to my youngest granddaughter of fourteen months. I had them all made in Xela.

All the guys wore suits. I bought an off-white, two-piece suit for myself. It was a beautiful wedding, all conducted bilingually for the benefit of Clarence, who did not speak Spanish, and for those who came from the United States. We had the civil wedding on Friday morning, July 11, and the church wedding on Saturday, July 12, 2003. The US did not recognize our marriage from Guatemala, so we had to have my local pastor in Caddo Mills conduct a two-minute ceremony so I could change my last name on all my legal documents. I've had three weddings to the same man. We have now been married for eighteen years. He has added so much to my life, family, and ministry. He is well loved and respected by the Guatemalan people.

Wedding of Clarence and me

Clarence's heart and passion is preaching the Word of God. Even though we have a local pastor, the people are always truly blessed when the Lord gives him a message to share with the congregation. He is the director of the work in Quetzaltenango, which entails working closely with the missionaries and the staff, giving advice, and sharing his wisdom. He is a trained and efficient carpenter and has been most of his life. He has built several pieces of furniture for our home and added a new patio and water fountain in the backyard. He built new cabinets for two missionary families and helped in various construction projects on the field. He stays on top of the financial accounts, teaches two courses in the Bible school, and speaks into the lives of the students during chapel sessions.

I count myself truly blessed. Living Water Teaching celebrated forty years of ministry in October 2019, to the glory of God. The celebration was awesome, and the church was packed. People we hadn't seen in years came. Together we celebrated the goodness and faithfulness of God. The vision is still strong, very much alive, full of life, and going forward in faith. The Lord has truly restored what the devil thought was the demise of Living Water Teaching.

I am a blessed wife and a happy mother of two grown women and one son in heaven. I currently have fifteen grandchildren and fifteen great-grandchildren. My life is full, and my love for the Guatemalan people continues to grow.

My famiy after the accident

We give all praise and glory to God that the ministry of Living Water Teaching continues. One of the Scriptures I stood on during the healing process is found in the first part of 2 Corinthians 2:14 (KJV): "Now thanks be unto God, which always causeth us to triumph in Christ."

Always. I took this Scripture literally for what it says. I took it by faith because at that moment, I was not triumphing in anything. I was too emotional to make any rational decisions. I became president of Living Water Teaching overnight, and it was a big job that I was not ready for. I had to fight against despondency and depression. These things are very real, and they can overtake you if you give into them. I needed to be strong for those around me and for my family. I stayed in church, in prayer, and in the Word of God. There were many times that I was overcome with grief, but it was in the privacy of my home. I did not want a spirit of grief to overtake me, so I would reject it and quote the Word. I knew that Jesus was my healer, and if this Scripture says "always," then I knew that it didn't mean once in a while, or frequently, or down the road. It meant "always." The Word of God is life, it is healing, and it causes us to triumph.

20

HOW TO OVERCOME ANYTHING THE ENEMY THROWS AT YOU

Jim and I were graduates of Rhema Bible Training Center in Broken Arrow, Oklahoma. Thanks be to God for the Word we received there. I stood on the Word to overcome this specific tragedy with triumph. It is important to learn how to stand before the Enemy strikes. As long as we live in this world, and as long as the devil is the god of this world, we are going to have opportunities for tests, trials, and afflictions.

But Jesus said in John 16:33, "These things have I spoken to you, that in Me you might have peace. In the world you shall have tribulation; but be of good cheer, I have overcome the world."

Our relationship and fellowship with our Father God and the Lord Jesus Christ is our victory.

Our attitude toward them is important. God is a good God all the time. He never changes. We can always be sure He is our Father, and He loves us. His will is to bless us. He always works for our good, and God is bigger than anything we go through.

Proverbs 24:10 (KJV) says, "If thou faint in the day of adversity, thy strength is small." When people go through a test, a trial, a divorce, an illness, or some other kind of tragedy, they should do several things in order to triumph:

1. Don't unplug from the Word of God. Keep the Word in the midst of your heart. Proverbs 4:22 says, "For they [His words] are life unto those that find them, and health to all their flesh." Speak the Word day and night. For example, *Lord, in 2 Corinthians 2:14, you said that you always cause us to triumph in Christ.* Likewise, Romans 8:37 says, "We are more than conquerors through Him who loved us." Deuteronomy 28:13 says, "And the Lord will make you the head and not the tail; you shall be above only, and not beneath."

2. Keep your faith strong. Don't cave in. First Corinthians 16:13 (KJV) says, "Watch ye, stand fast in the faith, quit you like men, be strong." Second Corinthians 1:24 says, "For by faith you stand." And in 1 John 5:4, the Word says, "This is the victory that has overcome the world, even our faith."

3. Do not yield to self-pity. Some say, "No one knows what I am going through." Personally, I did not want people to pity me. I wanted them to pray for me. Get around people who will encourage you and build you up, not those who say, "Oh, you poor thing. How awful for this to have happened." You must tap into God's love and praise Him—not for the affliction or problem you're going through but because He will take you through victoriously.

4. Do not blame God. We do not always know why things happen. I do not understand why the plane crashed, why eleven people went home early to be with the Lord, or why seven survived. I have never blamed God. But I do know that John 10:10 shows us we have an Enemy who has come to steal, kill, and destroy.

The Lord didn't speak to Jim and me about going to Guatemala until we had something to say and until we were trained in His Word. Your doctrine, your traditions, will never win the lost to Jesus. It is the gospel that is "the power of God unto salvation" (Romans 1:16 KJV).

I trust this book will be a blessing to you—a help, an encouragement, or an answer to what you might be going through.

Marion's son, Jimmy Zirkle

ORDER INFORMATION